Life's not Hollywood, it's Cricklewood

ERIC MORECAMBE

BY GARY MORECAMBE

Life's not Hollywood, it's Cricklewood

BBC BOOKS

Published by BBC Books, BBC Worldwide Limited
80 Wood Lane, London W12 0TT

First published 2003. Copyright © Gary Morecambe 2003
The moral right of the author has been asserted.

ISBN 0 563 48722 4

Commissioning editor: Ben Dunn
Project editor: Sarah Emsley
Copy editor: Ruth Baldwin
Designer: Annette Peppis
Picture research: David Cottingham
Production controller: Christopher Tinker

The extract from *Can You Tell What it is Yet?* by Rolf Harris, published by Bantam,
is used by permission of Transworld Publishers, a division of The Random House
Group Ltd.

BBC Books would like to thank the following for providing photographs and for
permission to reproduce copyright material. While every effort has been made to trace
and acknowledge all copyright holders, we would like to apologize should there have
been any errors or omissions.

Sections 1-3 Courtesy of the author
Section 4 © BBC
Except the following:
Section 1 page 8 ATV; 2 p4 Mirrorpix; 3 p5 (top right) *Sunday People*;
p6 (top) Thames TV; p8 Press Association.

Set in Sabon and Foundry
Colour separations by Radstock Reproductions, Midsomer Norton
Printed and bound in Great Britain by The Bath Press

Dedication

For my children, Jack, Henry, Arthur and Dereka. For making my life complete.

And thanks to David, Ken, Sean, Hamish, Toby and, of course, Eddie for bringing back the sunshine.

And Jo O'Callaghan for coming into my life and making me laugh again.

Acknowledgements

Thank you to everyone who contributed to this book.

Though it's been a personal exploration, other people have played their part. Thanks to Louise Webb for her help in understanding the psychology of Morecambe and Wise; to my agent, Jan Kennedy, and Suzanne Westrip at Billy Marsh Associates; to Felicity Trotman for her editing suggestions; to all at BBC Worldwide for making this such a pleasurable and memorable book to publish; and especially to Rupert Smith.

Eternal gratitude to my mother, Joan, sister, Gail, and brother, Steven, for being so cooperative and supportive of my endeavours to write this book, never once complaining or criticizing.

I should allow only my heart to have imagination, and for the rest rely on memory, that long-drawn sunset of one's personal truth.

Vladimir Nabokov

Fathers should neither be seen nor heard; that is the only proper basis for family life.

Oscar Wilde

contents

chronology

Eric Morecambe 1926–1984

1926
Born John Eric Bartholomew, 14 May. Only child of Sadie and George Bartholomew, Morecambe Bay, Lancashire.

1936
Joins cousin Peggy at Miss Hunter's dancing school in Morecambe. Creates a song-and-dance double act with local girl, Molly Bunting.

1938
Leaves school at the age of 12 to pursue a career in show business.

1939
Wins a talent competition organized by *The Melody Maker* and auditions for Jack Hylton in Manchester, where he meets Ernest Wiseman for the first time.

1941
Eric and Ernie appear as a double act for the first time billed as Bartholomew and Wise (Liverpool Empire). The same year EM changed his name to Eric Morecambe.

1943

Appears with Ernie in smash-hit show *Strike a New Note*.
Makes first radio appearance in *Youth Must Have Its Fling*.

1944

Called up and sent down the mines in Accrington as a Bevin
boy.

1945

Invalided out of mines with poor health and mild heart
trouble.

1946

Resumes double act with Ernie after chance meeting in
Regent Street, London.

1947

Tours with Ernie in Lord John Sanger's Circus and Variety
Tour.

1950

Morecambe and Wise sign with agent Frank Pope and begin
appearing regularly in Moss Empire Theatres.

1952

Marries Joan Bartlett, 11 December.

1953

Daughter, Gail, is born. Morecambe and Wise have their own
radio series, *You're Only Young Once*.

1954

Morecambe and Wise's first TV series for the BBC *Running Wild* is a flop.

1956

Son Gary is born. EM and Joan move into their first proper home in North Finchley, London. Morecambe and Wise return to television as guests on Winifred Atwell's show, scripts written by Johnny Speight.

1958

Morecambe and Wise tour Australia.

1960

Morecambe and Wise join agent, Billy Marsh.

1961

Morecambe and Wise's ATV series for Lew Grade begins. Eric and Ernie invited to appear on Royal Command Performance. Eric moves with his family to Harpenden, Hertfordshire.

1963

Morecambe and Wise win their first of six BAFTAs.

1964

The Beatles are guest stars on *The Morecambe and Wise Show*. Eric and Ernie make their first appearance on American television in *The Ed Sullivan Show* for CBS. First film *The Intelligence Men* filmed at Pinewood Studios.

1965

That Riviera Touch filmed at Pinewood and on location in the South of France.

1966

The Magnificent Two filmed at Pinewood.

1968

Morecambe and Wise smash all records in summer season at Great Yarmouth and leave ATV to join the BBC. November, Eric suffers first heart attack.

1969

Eric resumes performing. Wins BAFTA award. Eddie Braben becomes new scriptwriter for Morecambe and Wise.

1970

Voted Pipe-smoker of the Year. Becomes director of Luton Town Football Club. Wins BAFTA award.

1971

André Previn, Shirley Bassey and Glenda Jackson all make highly publicized debuts on *The Morecambe and Wise Show*. Wins BAFTA award. Honoured by the Radio Industries Organization.

1972

Wins BAFTA award.

1973

Adopts son Steven. Wins BAFTA award. Profiled by Kenneth Tynan in the *Observer Magazine*. Morecambe and Wise publish joint autobiography, *Eric and Ernie*.

1974

Honoured by Variety Club and Water Rats.

1976

Awarded the OBE, the Freedom of the City of London and an honorary degree by the University of Lancaster. Honoured by Variety Club. Father, George, dies.

1977

Mother, Sadie, dies. Becomes president of the Lord's Taverners. *The Morecambe and Wise Show* watched by record 28 million viewers.

1978

Morecambe and Wise join Thames Television. Former prime minister Harold Wilson is guest star on first Christmas show. Variety Club award.

1979

Suffers second heart attack. Undergoes bypass surgery. Appears in short film for Anglia TV based on works by poet laureate John Betjeman.

1980

Writes first novel, *Mr Lonely*, while recovering from bypass surgery. Appears in second short Betjeman film for Anglia TV.

1981

Morecambe and Wise voted into TV Hall of Fame.

1982

Writes *The Reluctant Vampire*, first children's novel.

1983

Writes *The Vampire's Revenge*, second children's novel. Records what will be the last ever Morecambe and Wise Christmas Show.

1984

Completes *Night Train to Murder*, a film destined to be his last work with Ernie Wise. Dies May 28 at the Roses Theatre, Tewkesbury.

1985

Stella, his second adult novel, completed by Gary Morecambe, published.

1987

The Illustrated Morecambe, by Gary Morecambe, published.

1990

Still on my Way to Hollywood, Ernie's autobiography, published.

1994

Behind the Sunshine, by Gary Morecambe and Martin
Sterling, published. BBC compile classic Morecambe and
Wise hosted by Ben Elton to mark tenth anniversary of Eric's
death. Tops the ratings.

1995

Blue plaque commemorating Eric put up by Comic Heritage
in London. Ernie announces retirement from show business
aged 70.

1996

Morecambe and Wise voted the favourite entertainers of all
time by television viewers' poll to mark sixty years of BBC
Television.

1998

Radio Times readers vote Morecambe and Wise the best TV
comedy stars of all time. *Morecambe and Wise,* by Graham
McCann, published. *Omnibus: The Heart and Soul of Eric
Morecambe* broadcast on BBC1.

1999

Ernie Wise dies, aged 73. Eric and Ernie each awarded a
posthumous BAFTA fellowship. Statue of Eric unveiled by
HM The Queen in Morecambe, Lancashire. Eric and Ernie
honoured with blue plaque in Pinewood Studios Hall of
Fame to commemorate their three films for The Rank
Organization.

2000
Internet poll votes Eric greatest British comedian of the twentieth century.

2001
ITV documentary *The Unforgettable Eric Morecambe*. David Pugh produces and Kenneth Branagh directs The Right Size in *The Play What I Wrote*, a tribute to Morecambe and Wise, at Wyndham's Theatre, London.

2002
Eric voted in at 32 in all-time Great Britons. *The Play What I Wrote* wins 2 Olivier awards.

2003
The Play What I Wrote opens to positive reviews on Broadway, New York, and is shortlisted for a Tony Award.

chapter I

I hadn't been born when Morecambe and Wise first surfaced as a double act at the Liverpool Empire in 1941, but I was walking and talking before they were stars. I was born in 1956; by the time I was five, Morecambe and Wise were on national television, and I began to realize that I had a famous father. I can dimly remember my sister Gail, who is two and a half years older than me, questioning EM about his fame one night when he'd come upstairs to kiss us goodnight. It was the moment when he went from being just my Dad to being someone special – when I became aware that there was something that marked our family out from ordinary people.

That was the beginning of a lifelong involvement with Morecambe and Wise, and since that moment I've never been able to divorce my life from theirs. Whether it's healthy to spend your life in the shadow of a famous parent is a matter of debate; I have never known any different, so I've come to accept the shadow as a friend. I have never known the total, blissful obscurity in which most children grow up. I've never fought against the fame, but that doesn't mean I've always embraced it. During my teen years the whole notion of belonging to a famous comedian's family rested uneasily on me – but we change, and times change, and by the time my father died in 1984 I'd come to enjoy the connection in a way, although it was many years before I felt able to talk openly about it, to let my secret slip during conversation.

The children of famous people have no choice in their destiny: the fame that they live with isn't theirs, it's just something they're born into. Reflected fame isn't real fame, and there are no rewards to balance the discomfort that it brings. The constant demands that were made on EM's time irritated me, but I soon realized that was always going to be part of our family life. Fortunately, my sister and brother and I grew up largely insulated from the world of show business; we were wheeled on for the occasional photo-shoot, but we were never obliged to do anything we didn't want to do. We lived as normal a life as my father's status would permit – and that was pretty normal, for the most part. EM wasn't one of those people who dwell on fame; he needed it, but he didn't let it consume him or his family. His genuine innocence about so many aspects of his career protected us from the more corrosive effects of fame.

I'm not famous, and I don't wish to be. My job is to promote the uniqueness of Morecambe and Wise at every suitable opportunity, and if, in doing so, that puts a focus on me as a writer, then that's a by-product I'm happy to accept. I enjoy promoting the work, but I'm not trying to score points off Morecambe and Wise. The attention I get is nice, and I'd be lying if I said I didn't like it, but it's not something I actively seek. That's the difference between me and my father. Also, he was a perfectionist. Living with one is not easy. I know that I found myself becoming the opposite of that, resentful of what striving for perfection both requires of and does to you.

Fame was a different thing in EM's time than it is today. For a start you had to possess a real talent and work very hard at proving how good you were. There was little chance of becoming the instant celebrity you now see emerging from programmes like *Big Brother*. It was also a time when people in the business trod the boards for many a long year honing their skills: programmes in which the public entertain the public just didn't exist.

I was an introverted child, shy and inhibited. Unlike EM I had no urge to perform; thank God he wasn't the sort of father who was determined to push his children out into the limelight. I was once given the lead role in the school play – which was in French, to make matters worse. Fortunately, which might sound an odd word to use, I developed glandular fever just in time to lose the part. The burden that was lifted from me was too immense to describe. I couldn't understand why anyone would want to learn lines, to dress up as someone else; all that EM embraced in his life, I rejected.

In private, though, I put on my own little performances, pretending to be Morecambe and Wise as I'd seen them on stage and television. My earliest memory of seeing them on TV is from 1961, when they'd just started their own series for ATV; I can't recall seeing any of their frequent guest appearances before that, but I have clear memories of their first ATV shows. I didn't understand any of the comedy, but I had a vivid and overwhelming fear that my father would walk off stage at the end of the show and disappear down a toilet. It was a real concern that genuinely troubled me, so much so that EM had to reassure me that nothing of the sort would happen, that the door that he went through at the end of every show just led to another part of the studio. It also worried me that my father was the funny, stupid one, who seemed endlessly to suffer; I found it hard to understand that he was playing a part.

I started to put on my own little versions of these shows on a sheet of wooden planking that lay in a field behind our house where the bulldozers had not yet moved in. For about three months it remained untouched, and I had a makeshift stage all to myself. I would do the crosstalk for both Eric and Ernie; I could envisage the footlights and the audience beyond. It was very real to me, especially when I stood there at the end of each performance, belting out their then theme song, 'Two of a Kind'.

I came out of my shell a bit at nursery school, probably because I was the only boy in the class, which gave me a sort of novelty value. I rather enjoyed showing off to the girls, and word would get back to EM that his son had made all the other kids laugh. On the rare occasions when he was free to collect me, he would quiz me all the way home about what I'd said that amused everyone so much. Perhaps he hoped that there was another little comedian in the family. The truth, however, was disappointing: I was the only boy, and so they thought I was inherently funny. When other little boys arrived, my comedy value plummeted, and I lost my audience.

My very early childhood was spent in a ground-floor flat in North Finchley, an outer suburb of London, near my maternal grandmother Alice's house in Whetstone; Mum's brother Alan ran a pub just down the road, the Torrington Arms, with his wife Pam. This flat was my parents' first proper home together, and we lived there till 1961, when EM's rising fortunes enabled them to buy their own house. In 1995 the entire Morecambe clan descended on the old North Finchley address, which has now been converted into a nursing home, to witness Comic Heritage attaching a blue plaque to the house to commemorate the fact that Eric Morecambe had lived there. It was a bittersweet experience for my mother, Joan, who smiled and said very little. It must have brought back so many memories of when she and EM had youth on their side, the war years comfortably behind them, an exciting future stretching ahead, and a young family to bring up. And now it was all over apart from the memories – and EM wasn't there to share them with her.

In 1961, when I was five, we moved to a brand-new house in Harpenden, Hertfordshire, some 20 miles north of London. It was a classy patch of suburbia, with endless developments in all styles and sizes being constructed around an increasingly complicated maze of streets, eating up the green fields that were fast disappearing beneath the crescents and avenues and drives of the prosperous, early sixties boom. I think my parents paid £5,000 to build their house, another £2,000 to furnish it. You couldn't buy the front door for that now; houses in that area are worth a king's ransom.

We could walk from our shiny new house through a lush green field of dwindling farmland and then discover, literally the next day, that the field had been turned over ready for the foundations of the next phase of building. Gail and I were excited by the diggers, and by the sense of newness and progress. The dourness of the post-war years was giving way to the growth of the sixties and, to paraphrase Mr Macmillan, we really had never had it so good. A rash of expensive homes sprouting across the countryside seemed much better than the countryside *au naturel*, and if that meant a few hundred hedgehogs becoming homeless, or a few thousand rabbits, or a few million insects, it didn't matter much. This was progress.

EM complained only once, when we lost a source of delicious wild mushrooms that grew in a field at the end of a concrete lane leading from our house. For two years we'd enjoyed the harvest – and there was a tragic air in the house on the day when the diggers moved in to rip up the field. I remember EM sighing, 'We'll have to buy our mushrooms from now on...' I think he missed the fields for less tangible reasons as well. Walking out there with my sister and me, he could feel that he was a thousand miles away from the TV studio; he forgot his work and enjoyed the countryside. EM found it hard to switch off from work; often when we were on holiday he'd disappear for most of the day to write new material and think about sketches. But out there, in the dwindling fields of Harpenden, he found it easy to relax, and he missed it when it was taken away from him.

Thinking of the year 1961 brings memories of sunny days in summer, running through the garden sprinkler with Gail while our dog, Chips, looked glumly on, and icy days in winter, with snowdrifts round the house and giant shark's teeth of icicles cracking in the watery afternoon sunlight. I recall EM's long absences and happy returns; when he was at home, he was really at home – it was like having a young unemployed man in the house, with nothing to do but give the children his full attention.

But as the sixties wore on EM was at home less and less. After struggling to break into television in the fifties, when they'd made one disastrous series for the BBC, *Running Wild*, Morecambe and Wise returned to the stage for a while before mustering all their energies for one last make-or-break assault on the small screen. They took every guest spot they could get, notably with Winifred Atwell and on *Sunday Night at the London Palladium*, and even managed to put together another short series of their own, *Double Six*. All of this hard work paid off when, in 1961, Lew Grade gave them their own show on ATV.

Morecambe and Wise remained his star performers until 1967, when they said their final, somewhat terse goodbyes and moved over to the BBC. ATV's *The Morecambe and Wise Show* was an instant hit, and before long they were making movies – *The Intelligence Men* (1965), *That Riviera Touch* (1966), *The Magnificent Two* (1967) – to capitalize on their TV fame. And they hadn't yet given up their stage work, so there were summer seasons and pantomimes to fit in between studio commitments. Hard graft was nothing new to Morecambe and Wise: they'd both been working, separately and together, since their teens, scratching a living on the variety circuit, getting radio slots when they could persuade a friendly producer, honing their act for fourteen years before they became TV stars. But now the stakes were higher, and for EM in particular the pressure was on. He was a workaholic who found it very difficult to switch off. Ernie was the more relaxed of the two, much more able to distinguish his working life from his home life. EM, as the funny man, rightly or wrongly felt much greater responsibility to carry the act, and it would be a lifelong source of stress that ultimately undermined his health.

By the time I started school *The Morecambe and Wise Show* – black and white, thirty minutes, scripts by Sid Green and Dick Hills – was fast becoming one of the biggest hits on TV. After their shaky start in television, they pulled it all together: their comic personae had begun to crystallize, and the classic bits of business – EM's glasses, the face-slapping, the strangling hand from behind the curtain – were all in place. Gail remembers seeing Eric and Ernie's faces beaming down from giant billboards along the roadside, and being aware that suddenly all her friends knew who our Dad was.

Gail, being a couple of years older than me, recalls a time before all of this, when Dad was just Dad, someone who worked hard, was away a lot, but was really no different from any other father. For me, EM's sudden transformation into a household name is tied up with my earliest memories. I never knew him any other way.

chapter   2

In many ways EM was a remote father figure to me – not just because, for most of my childhood, he was public property, but more to the point because he just wasn't around for a lot of the time. Right up until 1967 he and Ernie were working constantly, doing stage work when they weren't on TV, TV when they weren't on stage. If it was tough on me as a child, it was just as tough on EM as a father. When he was doing summer season, he'd install the family at whatever resort he was working in for as many weeks as possible, but as soon as the school holidays were over we'd go back to Harpenden and he'd be left on his own. It was easier for Ernie; he and his wife, Doreen, had chosen not to have children, and so she could be with him wherever he went. EM must have felt lonely; I know I would have done. He had all the highs that went with a big, responsive theatre audience, then he returned to the quiet of an empty room.

For a time in the sixties, EM kept a diary during his absences from home – just as a way of sharing some of his thoughts and feelings, I suppose, as he didn't have his wife and children with him. Mostly the diaries are chat about what he was doing, how the shows went, who he'd played golf with, plus occasional complaints about the weather or the food or the state of the nation. They're not profound diaries, and they offer no real insight into the way that Morecambe and Wise worked; they're merely the record of a very busy man working far from home, who half-wishes that he could be with his loved ones. Here's a typical extract from Yarmouth, August 1967:

> Both houses tonight are full, but the weather at the moment is good theatre weather. Friday and Saturday first houses could let us down and stop us from doing a burster – £9,900 – I think we might do around £9,500 this week. As for Yarmouth itself, although I'm making a lot of money here, I think it's the most terrible place. If cleanliness is next to Godliness, in Yarmouth it's next to impossible! Just outside the ABC stage door is a market, and at the end of the day there is so much newspaper and old fish and chips, as there are about six fish, chip and peas stalls belching out terrrible smells eighteen hours a day. But the public put up with all this dirt and smells. I've been reading papers lately about how dirty the British are – it seems to be true in Yarmouth.

No real reflection on Yarmouth – just a tired, lonely man letting off steam about the things that annoyed him. EM kept a diary for only one other year in his life, as far as I'm aware, and that was 1969, when he was recovering from his first heart attack, and once again was feeling bored, lonely and out of sorts with the world.

•

Family trips to see EM were always fun, and I remember the

1967 summer season in Yarmouth rather well. I was eleven
by now, and quite used to having a famous father and lots
of famous friends. Towards the end of August EM took us
all to lunch at Petersfield House Hotel at Horning, with
Arthur Askey, Val Doonican and his wife Lynn, and
Michael Grade, who at that time was working for EM's
agent, Billy Marsh. It was a glorious day, the meal was
excellent, and we finished up with tea and champagne on
the lawn. EM noted in his diary that 'Gail and Gary were
extra-well-behaved', which would have given him great
pleasure: like his own parents, he set great store by good
behaviour in children. We were on pain of death if we
misbehaved.

Lunch was a slow, formal, adult affair, which was very
boring for a child, but once the meal was out of the way we
did have some fun. I remember fooling around with Arthur
Askey, who was pleasingly no taller than I was, and being
taken out in a motor boat. EM was very attached to Askey,
who had been a star when he and Ernie were working their
way up in the business; Ernie, of course, had worked as a
child star with Askey back in the early forties. I could never
see anything funny about what Arthur Askey did, but EM
always had huge respect for him, partly because he was
someone who'd been around even longer than he had. I'd
meet Arthur again many times during my working life, and he
was always very kind to me because of who my father was.

EM loved this kind of event, when he was surrounded by
his peers and his family, when he could perform to an
audience with whom he felt completely at home. But there
was never any doubt that he was performing. EM was

always performing, on stage, at social functions, at home. He never stopped. My father was a comedian – all the time. He could never switch off. During my early childhood, I accepted this as a fact of life, but as time went on it began to strike me as strange and irritating. It got to the point where I would constantly be looking over my shoulder, expecting EM to make a surprise entrance, or do a funny gag. That was much later, though; for now it all seemed like innocent fun.

Much as EM enjoyed a party, our home life was fairly quiet. EM and Joan were invited to functions galore, and they had hundreds of acquaintances in their show-business circle, but their intimate social life was on a very small scale. Our house was never the centre of party life. They weren't great entertainers; I've often thought that this provided a balance for EM's professional life, in which he was permanently entertaining. They would have people round for lunch, and occasionally for drinks, but beyond that they kept a low profile. My showbiz memories from the sixties all take place outside the home; back in Harpenden it was just Mum, Dad, Gail and me – and Chips the dog. Chips was the family's first pet, a small terrier who had a love-hate relationship with EM. To be more exact, it was a hate-hate relationship. EM tried to be nice to the dog, but he was also very wary of him, and Chips had a tendency to snap at him without warning. In the end EM gave up trying, and would just wander into the kitchen where Chips was lying in his basket, point a finger and say, 'Die, Chips! Die!' – which he eventually did, although not to oblige EM. Chips was succeeded by Barney, a rather energetic golden retriever, of whom EM was far fonder. But overall, he just wasn't a pet person. The only animals he got any real pleasure from were the tropical fish he kept in a tank in his study during the later years of his life.

Gail liked horses, and he seemed to tolerate them enough to buy her one. He would occasionally be spotted feeding it a sugar lump, but generally he kept his distance, certain that, as writer Ian Fleming put it, 'They're dangerous at both ends and uncomfortable in the middle.' His fears were borne out when Gail had an appalling fall from her horse, losing her front teeth and breaking her nose and jaw. The accident occurred only hours after EM had returned from working in the States, and totally disorientated him. Gail spent the afternoon at the hospital, and when she went to bed that night EM went to look in on her. Thinking she was asleep, he sat on the bed and sobbed and sobbed. Gail says she can remember the bed gently vibrating as he cried.

Sometimes I'd put on little shows for my parents with my prized Chad Valley projector, which shone still images of Yogi Bear and Huckleberry Hound on to my bedroom walls. Mum and Dad would dutifully climb the stairs and sit in the dark watching these for twenty minutes, while I played the usherette and handed out snacks consisting of a digestive biscuit with a fruit gum on top. They would both eat their biscuits, but I was always pleased when EM said, 'I think I'll leave the sweet till later' – because then he'd 'forget' it and I could eat it instead.

During their ATV years Morecambe and Wise released a record called 'We're the Guys', with which I became totally obsessed. EM had bought me a little Dansette record player, and I'd sit in my room playing the song over and over until even EM would stick his head round the door and say, 'You must be fed up with it by now...' His expression was a mixture of pain from the endless repetition and pride that he'd achieved such a hit with his son. Other records that used to sound through that house included Bert Weedon's 'High Steppin'' and 'Tokyo Melody', Buddy Greco's 'They Can't Take That Away From Me', and the early Beatles.

Football played a big part in our lives at that time. This was before EM had fallen in love with Luton Town FC; in those days he talked about Preston North End and Manchester United, of the grounds he visited in his youth, full of cloth caps and trenchcoats, of clouds of Woodbine smoke and throaty coughs. In 1966 we watched the World Cup final together, and I seem to have a vivid memory of the bright red shirts of the England team, the yellow, flailing hair of Bobby Charlton, the deep gold of the cup held aloft by a suntanned Bobby Moore – all of this from a black-and-white TV set in the corner of our living room.

Football was one of our great garden sports, with jumpers as goalposts and EM unable to resist hogging the ball. He'd keep up a running commentary: he was either Eusebio of Portugal or Bobby Charlton. Either way he always seemed to have possession. Being in goal wasn't much fun – EM had a vicious left foot and sometimes he'd have a rush of blood to the head and let rip with its full power. He always fancied himself as a footballer, and, like his father before him, had intended going for trials. Injury put an end to his father's footballing career; comedy put an end to EM's.

On summer afternoons we'd play cricket in the garden, and I can still smell the linseed oil on my bat with the disintegrating string handle. And there was the compound ball that EM would gleefully toss down the garden towards me with plenty of deliberate spin. I was always asking him, 'Why can't we use a real cricket ball, Dad?' and he'd say, 'Because it might hurt if it hits you, and you haven't got pads.' Compound or not, it still bloody well hurt when it missed the bat and struck the shin. EM, in the excitement of appealing for LBW, wasn't especially bothered about that.

Sometimes my friends would come round to play cricket with us, and that was always a relief; having others on the team lessened the intensity of those one-on-one games with EM. An injured shin from an LBW could be treated at the time, without interrupting the flow of EM's game. He was less impatient and restless when we had a 'real' game, as he called it, on our hands. He even allowed us to pause for a glass of orange squash without his usual frustrated sighs.

There was a strange streak of cruelty in my father, which I find hard to reconcile with his generally sunny disposition. He was highly competitive, even with his own children. Gail recalls how she was practising the piano one morning, working really hard on a Chopin prelude that she'd been studying, and EM came downstairs and said, 'That was really good, Gail. I thought I was listening to the radio.' Then he sat down next to her at the piano and said, 'But can't you play something like this?' And he proceeded to play a wonderful jazz improvisation on the prelude, something that Gail would never have been able to do in a thousand years. She had to practise hard with the music in front of her in order to play anything; EM could just toss it off without any effort. He was impatient with anything that didn't come naturally. I am sure that one of the reasons he gave up playing golf is that he didn't have a gift for it, and he wasn't willing to put in the practice.

EM took pleasure in asking Gail and me, 'Who do you love more, me or your Mum?' He saw it as a bit of lightheartedness, I suppose, and we would invariably conclude that we loved them both equally, but at the time – particularly the first time he asked us – it really troubled us. Michael Sellers, Peter Sellers's son, has told me that his father used to ask the same thing. Perhaps it was a result of insecurity, of craving approval, or perhaps it was just leg-pulling, but either way there's an element of cruelty in subjecting a child to that sort of question. EM was oblivious to any pain inflicted by words; in his own mind he was just pulling our legs, and so the pain couldn't be real. I remember being angry with him for the first time.

Our upbringing was quite strict. I've said how important good behaviour was, and this extended to our appearance as well. Gail and I were always well scrubbed and well turned out. I would be wearing a pair of shiny grey shorts, white stocking socks, a crisp white shirt and an elasticated bow tie. I've had a horror of bow ties ever since; my mother has lots of photographs of me in this uniform, and they never fail to make me shudder. Gail had to wear bonnets and lacy white gloves, which looked smart but were not very practical. We must have made a striking picture: Mum always looked incredible – she had been a model and she always looked like one. Nobody would have guessed that she didn't have a nanny, a domestic and an au pair to help her keep everything so spick and span, but in truth it was all her own work; there wasn't a lot of money around in those days, and my parents would never have dreamed of borrowing any.

We learned fast that looking good and behaving well was a sure way of getting praise from EM. On the way home from a garden party or a fête, Dad would glow with pride. 'Well, kids, you were really good today. People told me what wonderfully behaved children I have.' We wanted his approval, and we didn't want to let him down. I don't think we ever rebelled.

In retrospect, it strikes me that EM was a shallow and selfish person in his expectations of his children. Even allowing for the era – we're talking forty years ago – it still somehow grates with me. There's something so lacking when the winning formula is down to behaviour and the smartness of one's clothes.

EM instilled very strong morals into us as children. He taught by parables, and the story of the lion was a special favourite. A man is walking in the wild and he meets a lion that's in pain. Instead of running away, the man takes pity on the lion and removes a thorn from its paw. Years later the man is captured by the Romans and thrown into the arena to fight for his life. The lion sent in to fight him recognizes the man and won't kill him. 'Do someone a good turn,' EM would say, 'and one day they'll be good to you in return.' He also used to tell us about the man who was sad because he had no shoes, 'until one day,' said EM, 'he met a man who had no feet.'

Every so often EM would get up to real mischief. In the days before traffic jams and seat belts he would let me sit on his lap in the car and steer us home down back roads. On one occasion we passed the milkman, who stopped dead in his tracks when he saw this five-year-old 'driving' a car; he couldn't see the adult hiding beneath.

And ten years later, on that very same stretch of road, EM suggested that I should buy a razor, as the first shadow of downy hair was appearing on my face. Ten years; it felt like ten minutes.

chapter 3

In 1964 I started going to prep school. I can still taste the dryness in the throat that accompanied a thousand breakfasts, as another day of fighting for survival at school began. Those were the hurt, sad, worried times of my childhood – but the pain was short-lived, and I don't think any lasting damage was done. So was school that tough? No, probably not. Just the standard all-boys preparatory school of the sixties, which was tough enough for a nervous, inhibited lad with a father whom everyone recognized.

Having a famous father set me apart from the other children; not in a physical sense, because we were all chucked in together, but in the sense that I was easily labelled. Later in life it seemed quite cool to have a famous Dad, but back then it was definitely uncool, and I was duly embarrassed about having a 'clown' for a father. That was the word they used, with comments to the effect that it was a shame my father couldn't get a real job. It crossed my mind that my father was probably making a lot more money than their fathers, and having a more interesting life to boot, but I said nothing and responded with a plaintive nod of the head. I learned quickly that you go along with your peers even if they're wrong – unless you want a black eye or a sharp punch in the stomach.

I got both, but that was more to do with the politics of the playground than my famous father. In fact I was really proud of what EM was doing, and the more records he made, the more radio, stage and TV appearances, the greater the pride. But at that early stage in my life, I had to stifle it. Rare were the youngsters around me who rejoiced in my father's success, and I wasn't looking for trouble. I suppose it was jealousy on their part. After all, there weren't many kids who got dropped off at school in a Rolls-Royce.

In 1968 I started boarding at prep school as a way of acclimatizing me to the boarding that lay ahead at senior school. Despite the prevailing negative attitude to my Dad, there was always a certain amount of excitement when he came to the school to see me in a school play (I did occasionally allow myself to be talked into appearing) or a sports day. I was conscious of the other parents thinking, 'That's Eric Morecambe's son – and that's Eric Morecambe, watching his son.' It's the same for my children now when I go to watch them at school, such is the power of the Morecambe and Wise legacy. I know exactly how they feel. I went to collect my youngest son, Arthur, from school one evening, and on a table was a copy of the 'Weekend' section of the *Mail on Sunday* with a huge colour picture of Eric and Ernie on the cover. 'I told my friend that it was a picture of my Grandad,' said Arthur, 'but he didn't believe me.'

One abiding memory of EM at my prep school concerns the annual sports day. EM and Joan, like most parents, had come to cheer me along, and although I was no athlete I was running in what would now be called the 800 metres. I knew in advance that if I didn't come last, I'd come second from last, and EM knew that too. 'Never mind,' he said, 'I've got my camera, so get off to a good start, and I'll get some nice shots while you're in the lead.' It was a good plan, and its Baldrick-like cunningness appealed to me. I set off at a sprint, and held the lead for about 300 metres; by then, EM had taken lots of shots. As I crawled in breathless and last, he came over and patted me on the back. 'No problem!' he said. 'It's all on film!'

A week later I went home on a break. 'Have you developed the photos, Dad?' A sheepish EM delayed a moment, then said, 'Ah. Yes. Well, it seems there was a problem with the camera...' So no photos of me 'winning' the 800 metres at sports day.

And in 1968 we were on the move again. Morecambe and Wise had left ATV after six and a half successful years, and in that year they started working for the BBC. Coincidentally we were moving house at the same time, and it must have seemed as if EM had felt that with the change in channels, he should also have a change in houses. Mum and Dad had started the Lew Grade era in 1961 with a brand-new house; now EM was a big name, and in a sense it felt as if we were celebrating the fact. Our second house in Harpenden was just a mile down the road, but it was much more spacious and private, and the previous owner had dug a large muddy hole in the ground that would eventually be transformed into a swimming pool, full of iridescent blue water and splashing, laughing children. The move to the new house is still very clear in my mind; I was twelve, and to me that's the dividing line between the two eras of my childhood.

I would live at this house almost non-stop until I was twenty-two, but whenever I visit it now I seem to be visiting a house that's connected with someone else's life, not mine – or an entirely different me, one that might have existed in a book or a film. It's a home still – my mother continues to live there – but it's also a shrine. It's where I go to collect photos of Morecambe and Wise for books like this one. It's where I can see all their awards lining the window ledges and burying the baby grand piano. It was my base, where my bed lay unmade, and now it's my mother's home, where I visit her, and my past, the past we shared with EM. It was EM's home at the time of his death, although he didn't die there, and so for me the traumatic events of that time permeate the bricks and mortar of the place, a shower on a day otherwise filled with sunshine.

•

In between memories of home and school, there are flashes of visits north to stay with my paternal grandparents, Sadie and George, in Lancashire. Sadie – Mrs Sarah Bartholomew – was a remarkable woman. She'd been born in the wrong place at the wrong time; in another life, she might have revealed her artistic side. She had a sharp mind and endless conversation, she was a good listener as well as a good talker, and she was just someone you enjoyed being around, without quite being able to say why. I think it's because she had a great soul. But there weren't many opportunities for a woman born in the north of England at the beginning of the twentieth century, and so Sadie grew old doing what she'd been born to do – she married, she kept house and she had a child. It was on that one child, John Eric Bartholomew, that she lavished all her love and ambition.

George did what he was born to do as well: he married, he became a father, and he worked securely for the local council for most of his life. He, too, was trapped by his times, but it didn't perturb him; George genuinely liked a quiet life and had little ambition. I remember him as always being on the verge of smiling, always whistling some familiar song, rarely in tune. He liked to banter endlessly; nonsense was his trademark, and it was only in later years that I realized what a lot of rubbish he'd fed me over the years. Best of all he liked a nonsense song, some of which I can still recite.

> Down in a sewer
> Shovelling up manure
> All amongst the piddle and the plop,
> There were roars of delight
> As he shovelled up the shite
> All amongst the piddle and the plop.

George was a character; he'd once owned a circus dog that wouldn't settle at night until it had had a smoke on his pipe. He was a tall, good-looking man with an Errol Flynn moustache and what Sadie used to call 'film star looks'. He loved dancing, and Sadie didn't, but she was quite happy to let him go out week after week with his regular dancing partner. I can still remember him now, doing the soft-shoe shuffle around the kitchen while making himself a cup of tea. When EM was little, George had an accident and broke his leg very badly; the doctors wanted to amputate, but he refused. Sadie had to return to work while George stayed at home and looked after the house and the baby; there weren't many men at that time who would have been prepared to do that.

Sadie was the stronger personality, and she was extremely focused. She identified her son's talent, and she realized that it could lead to a fuller, more rewarding future for him, so she pushed and pushed until he made it. I wonder whether, left to his own devices, EM would have bothered about the long grind to stardom had that maternal encouragement been lacking; perhaps he would have turned out more like his father, content to talk nonsense to a small circle of adoring grandchildren.

But Sadie wasn't the archetypal showbiz mum, grabbing at glory through the talents of her child. She had long ago accepted her lot, and she liked it too, but she still believed that she could give her boy a push along the road while youth and opportunity were in his hands. She was a confident, perceptive personality who would not easily accept defeat. She could take the knocks, and show business always has plenty of knocks to hand out. Whatever happened to EM, Sadie always got him back on track, and if she'd lived for longer she'd have been the first person I turned to whenever I needed help. She was logical, patient and pragmatic, and she always knew a good opportunity when she saw one.

And she saw one very good opportunity coming EM's way in 1939, when he was visiting the Manchester Odeon to audition for the impresario and talent-spotter, Jack Hylton. There was another young man waiting to rehearse, a sharp-featured little blond called Ernie Wise. The two young hopefuls exchanged no more than a nod backstage, but on the way home Sadie said, 'That's Ernie Wise. He's worked with Arthur Askey.' The next time their paths crossed, in Swansea in 1940, where both were working for Hylton, Sadie took Ernie under her wing and encouraged their budding friendship. She also noticed, as they toured the country together, that there was a good deal of gagging and back-chatting going on between the two – and it was Sadie who first suggested that they should form a double act.

It was a gradual process; Jack Hylton had employed two solo acts, not a double act, but his right-hand man Bryan Michie supported the lads and gave them a break. As long as they both did their solo spots, they were allowed to come on for a few minutes as a double act, and the date for their first try-out was the Liverpool Empire in August 1941. The momentous decision to change Eric's name was taken on a train some miles outside of bomb-flattened Coventry. Goodbye, John Eric Bartholomew from Morecambe and hello, Eric Morecambe of Morecambe and Wise.

They plodded on through 1941 and 1942 until the war got in the way: Ernie was called up into the Merchant Navy and EM was sent down the mines as a Bevin boy. It wasn't until 1947 that they met up again, when both were booked as solo turns in Sanger's Circus Show, and the double act was re-formed. Without Sadie's vision and support, it would never have happened at all.

I can see Sadie now, standing in the kitchen peeling a bucket of Morecambe Bay prawns for our tea. How she did it with such dexterity I will never know; years of practice, I suppose. I remember evenings when we ate chips wrapped up in newspaper, before it was considered unhygienic to put food directly on yesterday's newsprint. The paper would soak up the vinegar like a sponge, and recalling the combination of smells makes my mouth water as I write. A fountain of salt on the table, enough to block every major artery, all washed down with a fizzy apple-juice drink. George kidded me that it was wine.

George got off to work every morning at 6.30 after a breakfast of fried bread; if Gail and I got up quickly enough, he'd do some for us as well. Then he'd be on his bicycle with trouser clips and a beret, very Frank Spencer.

EM and George and Sadie would try to play cards, all cheating and all knowing that the others were cheating, no one winning because the game would erupt into accusations and teasing and laughter. The same with bagatelle; if you turned your back for a moment, the balls would have been shifted into higher-value pockets.

Sadie would tell me stories of EM's childhood, with EM constantly sticking his head round the door saying, 'It's all lies.' Sadie would wave him away, saying, 'Keep out of this. You were too young to remember.' Sadie and Eric shared barbed conversation in a typical northern mother-and-son manner. Sadie: 'Enjoy your money while you've got it. You can't take it with you.' Eric: 'Not where you're going – it'll only melt.' It was all a tease, but sometimes I wondered if there wasn't a little gentle retribution being meted out by EM for all the dance classes and talent contests he went through, all the encouraging, all the cajoling and controlling. He always acknowledged that he was grateful for it, but you can be grateful for all kinds of things in this world and still resent them. Sadie had been his guiding light, and he had achieved way beyond either his or Sadie's expectations. 'You were right,' he'd say, 'but it wasn't easy. I was the one having to walk off to the sound of my own footsteps at the Glasgow Empire, not you!'

During EM's formative years as a performer, right up to (and possibly after) his marriage to my mother, Sadie made him keep detailed records of income and expenditure. In the faded book I have, there are entries like: 'INCOME: second week in panto: 30 shillings. EXPENSES: cigarettes, 1/6. Bus fares, 3/-.'

In the era from which Morecambe and Wise emerged, you dealt in hard-earned cash and nothing else. You lived totally within your means. Luxury was not starving.

chapter 4

Nobody could have sustained the kind of workload that EM was subjecting himself to in the sixties without paying the price. In his 1967 Yarmouth diary EM noted:

> 14 September. Happy Birthday, Gail. Fourteen years. My, how time flies. It's nice to have a son and a daughter, and they are both good children. I think I must be one of the luckiest men alive! I've got a wonderful wife, two great children, houses, a hotel, money – almost everything! Sometimes it worries me – I feel something's got to give. I know what Harry Secombe meant when he said he's worried that one day the phone will ring and a very mystic voice will say, 'Thank you, Mr Secombe. Now can we have it all back?'

The call was not long in coming.

> 19 September. Went home at the weekend, started off at 7am, two hours and 25 minutes... Had pains in my arms, which could be indigestion. Had them off and on for some weeks now. Hell of a long time for indigestion...

Today, of course, these pains would have been recognized as

the early warnings of heart disease, but in 1967 EM believed that cardiac arrests were something that only happened to old people. Looking back, however, it is easy to identify him as a prime candidate: he was in his forties, he worked too hard in a highly stressful career, and he smoked heavily – although, at this time, he was trying to switch from cigarettes to a pipe.

There are further sporadic references to chest pains throughout 1967, but EM didn't take it too seriously; he was by nature a hypochondriac, and could spend hours with like-minded friends discussing his symptoms. Perhaps he thought that the chest and arms pains were nothing more than another twinge. He visited a doctor while he was in Yarmouth, but there's no mention of any serious alarm. Perhaps the doctor just told him to get more rest and cut down on smoking.

In retrospect, it's easy to see the signs. EM was increasingly irritable throughout 1967 and into 1968, finding fault with everything – and it was a pattern that repeated itself in the build-up to his two subsequent heart attacks in 1979 and 1984. But he kept on working at the same unforgiving pace, focusing his energies on his new BBC show, his stage work, his family and his new house, which was constantly being extended and improved during this time. To add to the stress, EM and Joan had bought a house in Portugal a couple of years earlier, and were also partners in a hotel business in Cambridge run by Joan's brother, Alan. Something had to give.

It was during an engagement in Batley, Yorkshire, in November 1968, that the hints of the previous year gave up hinting and struck in one big blow. EM suffered a near-fatal heart attack, and no one knew for sure what the future would bring. He was only forty-two, but it seemed for a while as if his life was over.

I was at boarding school when EM had his heart attack; when I came home, he had returned from hospital in Leeds, and he seemed to me to have been transformed from my father to my grandfather in one fateful night. Suddenly I was living with a man who wasn't allowed to walk up the stairs, who couldn't sit through too much television or read a demanding or over-stimulating book, who couldn't play football, or be hugged or squeezed. He was a dependant. A typical extract from his diary at this time shows how sedentary his life had become:

> It's been a very quiet day. Very nice and I've rested today. No walking. I feel very well – I hope it lasts. Ernie's brother Gordon rang today – he's going to farm in Rutland somewhere so I hope I'll see something of him. He said he might be able to fix me up with some fishing – I really do hope so. It's good around there.
>
> Anyway, I'm now watching an old 'terror' film on TV. Oh dear! It was made a hundred years ago! It's so old, a car drives in central London and parks!

It was a nightmare for my mother, whose shock was as great as mine but whose responsibilities in the future would be considerably greater. All that was required from us children was to be quiet and considerate.

My mother expressed her concern about our finances in

one simple mother-to-son conversation. I came up with what I thought was a good solution.

'You can stop my pocket money if it helps.'

My mother resisted a smile and said, very diplomatically, 'That won't be necessary for a while. But thank you.'

One memory that will always stay with me is EM's own father, George, saying, 'He's too young! It should have been me!'

Whatever EM and Joan's concerns for their future, the immediate effects of the heart attack were rather good for Gail and me. Our father changed: he became calmer, slower, more introspective. He enjoyed life more – and he spent a great deal more time with us at home:

Well, today was one of the best days since the heart attack. First of all I drove the Jensen car to Coldecote Farm at Bushy taking Gail to see Melody, her horse. She had a good ride. Also Father came with me in the car – it's the first time I have driven and I really enjoyed it. This afternoon I took Joan to Harpenden shopping.

EM would never descend entirely from the treadmill, but he made some significant changes to his working life, realizing that his workload had been at least partly responsible for the failure in his health. I suppose he might have considered giving up altogether, and it must have been a period of terrible uncertainty for Ernie and Doreen, but he was soon keen to get back to it:

Johnny Ammonds, our BBC TV producer, rang, and after

asking if I was all right asked if I could do a TV bit for one of our own programmes as the BBC want to do a 'Best of Morecambe and Wise'. I jumped at the idea. So I should be back on TV late Feb. I'm looking forward to that. It will not be hard – it will only be a small compering bit to one of our own shows, sat down (if I wish) and no audience. Great. This is the best way to creep in – or back...

EM realized that he would now have to work in a much more structured way. No more summer seasons or winter pantos. Less guesting at this and that, fewer openings of this shop or that fete. No more frantic half-hour shows recorded live. The forty-five-minute shows that Morecambe and Wise were recording for the BBC were much less stressful affairs, with plenty of time for rehearsal, all smoothly organized by Bill Cotton, the head of light entertainment.

At home EM was now more available than at any previous time. In the summer holidays we'd sit together and watch Wimbledon, taking bets on who was going to win – and inevitably EM would pick the player who would be knocked out in the second round. We'd sit around the pool, sometimes with friends, more often just the family, and EM would bring down his tape machine and put on one of his home-recorded cassettes, something like Roger Miller ('King of the Road') whom he loved. EM would sit in the pool in an inflated dinghy, a drink in one hand, his meerschaum pipe in the other, billowing smoke. One day he dozed off and burnt a hole in the side of the dinghy. It made a loud farting noise and began to sink. EM, who couldn't swim, woke up and started shouting 'Help!', struggling to the side of the pool entangled in deflated yellow rubber and canvas. I had to walk away from the scene; he wouldn't have liked to see his own son falling about with laughter at his predicament. EM liked to orchestrate the laughs he got, not achieve them through some genuine misfortune.

Sometimes he'd sit by the pool with his friend Gordon Beningfield, the countryside artist, who, like EM, was a great hypochondriac. The two of them could spend hours comparing medical histories, trying to outdo each other's aches and pains. Any pain Gordon had, EM had worse. Now and then I would chip in with a pain of my own – yes, I've continued the Morecambe hypochondria tradition – but I was never taken seriously. I had youth on my side, and anything I was suffering was just a growing pain. I couldn't be *really* ill like they were!

Gail saw a lot more of EM than I did. I was boarding now, whereas she was going to Winkfield Place, a Cordon Bleu finishing school, living at home and commuting into London every day. She remembers EM coming home tense from rehearsals, sitting quietly in the playroom with a cup of tea to unwind for five minutes, then relaxing into his usual genial self. He'd sit and joke with Gail and Joan, and it became a very special time of day for the three of them. I missed out on all of that – and, because EM recorded the shows at the weekend, I often didn't see him during my home visits either.

•

EM's heart attack made him revise his whole attitude to his career. He became a lot less driven; I suppose he realized that he'd made it now in any case, and there was no longer any need to crucify himself in order to achieve success. His convalescence gave him a chance to reflect on life, and for the first time in twenty years he took stock of his professional position. He'd been working constantly in that time, always chasing the next opportunity, striving to take the next step up the ladder, facing the next challenge – theatre, radio, television, films, records. Now he looked around him and realized that he'd climbed a very big mountain, and that he was near the top. In the next few years he'd climb even higher, until by the mid-seventies he and Ernie were uncontestably the most popular entertainers in the country. But the hard climb was done; they were above the clouds, out in the sunshine, and it was time to relax a little and enjoy it.

How much EM did enjoy his success, though, I've never been too sure. Certainly he liked the material benefits – the pool and the cars, the nice houses and holidays. But his attitude towards his career and what it brought him remained ambivalent throughout his lifetime. The stigma of being a 'clown' never brought him pleasure, nor did the nagging suspicion that some day he would be 'found out', that the public would no longer be fooled or enchanted by his mugging and gagging, and that his success would evaporate. In his more sanguine moments EM was aware of the real worth of what he was doing: life, he would say, is a tragedy that's constantly unfolding around us, and he was cast as the fool whose job it was to lighten the load that we all bear. That's about as far as he ever went towards analysing his comic gifts.

Gail remembers walking into the living room one day to find EM beaming all over his face. She asked him what he was grinning at, and he said that he had just heard someone describe him as a 'comic genius'. 'Isn't that hilarious?' he said, and just laughed it off. He didn't think deeply about his talent. He used to say, 'Don't try and analyse it. I do what I do, and if I start trying to work out where it comes from or why I'm funny, I'll go mad or depressed or both.' He thought this was what had happened to Tony Hancock, with horrifying results.

A few years later I'd have discussions with EM about Morecambe and Wise; he always referred to them in the third person – 'What Morecambe and Wise do', 'the thing about Morecambe and Wise', and so on. I asked him once if he thought he was a comic genius; it was a fair question, because so many people said that he was. 'That's for others to decide,' he said. 'I do what I do to the best of my ability, and I think I'm good at it. I know how to get laughs. But I haven't really suffered. Spike Milligan is a comic genius in my book, because he has suffered for his art.' And we left it at that. There was no point in pressing EM on a subject he felt uncomfortable about. He felt that he had no 'dark side'; perhaps he felt that this meant there was something lacking in his comedy. To him, the word 'genius' applied only to those troubled souls like Peter Sellers, Spike Milligan, Tommy Cooper, W. C. Fields, right back to the suicidal Dan Leno. EM's genius, if genius it was, was not of that order. His comedy was not introspective or troubling. But that doesn't mean it was any less great.

Part and parcel of this ambivalent attitude to his success was a delight in not being recognized in public. By the time Morecambe and Wise moved to the BBC in 1968, it was rare for EM to go anywhere without people approaching him to say hello; he didn't mind, but I don't think he ever particularly liked it. I remember accompanying him to a radio interview once, and we were greeted in reception by an austere-looking woman of indeterminate years, who looked at us over steel-rimmed glasses.

'Yes?'

'I'm Eric Morecambe. I'm here to do an interview.'

'I see. And how are we spelling that?'

EM loved these bizarre moments. 'She's probably the only person left in the country who's never watched a television,' he chuckled as we made our way to the lift.

Sometimes EM moaned about the restrictions of fame, about how he couldn't go out without being recognized, but he was the first to acknowledge that things would have been much worse if nobody spotted him at all. Fundamentally he enjoyed being famous because it represented the fruits of his labour. Fame meant that all those years of treading the boards, of slogging away to get on radio and TV, had been worth it. That's why, generally speaking, he made an effort to be nice to the autograph-hunters who approached him in the street; he felt that their attention was just a recognition of his success.

One Christmas EM had been a guest on some kind of festive programme with Roy Castle, and we were on our way home to our own celebrations when a very elderly lady approached the car just as EM switched on the engine. She said, 'I just wanted to thank you for the happiness and love you have brought into my life.' I was a bit embarrassed, but EM was visibly overcome. He smiled warmly, but it was a bit of a strain. And when she kissed his hand, he said, 'That's very, very kind. That's the nicest thing I've heard. You've made my Christmas.' We drove away in silence. After a couple of minutes, he said, 'She's thanking me! It's me that should be thanking her...'

I think that old lady hit the nail on the head: Morecambe and Wise were all about love. Their love of entertaining, their love of their audiences, the love that imbued their theme song: 'Bring me fun, bring me sunshine, bring me love!'. He would never have said this himself, but I think EM agreed with that old lady.

'The Beatles got it right,' he used to say. 'All you need is love.'

chapter 5

In 1969, at the age of thirteen, I moved up to my senior school, Aldenham School near Elstree, Hertfordshire, where I stayed until 1973. The day before I had to pack my trunk and go, EM took me on a birdwatching walk – one of the few interests which, along with fishing, he never tired of. It was a sunny afternoon, and he asked me along to carry his camera. We walked down a track beyond the garden which bisected the golf course; it was a familiar route, one which both Gail and I had taken often with him, although rarely together. On this particular afternoon we were on our own, and school wasn't mentioned; my stomach was already knotted with stress as it was.

It was a beautiful September day, but I knew that my life would never be the same again. I was about to take a decisive step away from the innocence of my childhood, and the tranquil beauty of that afternoon intensified the feeling of imminent change. Something that, for a long time, had been locked away in the future was about to become the present. I felt hollow and hopelessly alone. I felt as if I was being called up to go to war. Sights, sounds and scents were all enhanced by the thought.

The memory of that last afternoon of freedom is

immortalized by a single photograph that EM took of me, and which I include in this book. Whenever I glance at it, I am transported back to that moment, to the gentle conversation, the freedom I was about to be denied. I'm smiling in the photo, but it's a false smile. I felt utterly condemned. And I couldn't explain how I felt, at least not to EM, as he had not only never experienced boarding school, but by my age had already left school. School, to EM, was never more than somewhere to go for a quiet smoke. All he recognized about private schools was that they were expensive, and it followed that they were guaranteed to give me something he had not been fortunate enough to have.

That's undoubtedly true; EM escaped school, because of the times and the circumstances in which he grew up, but he was unbelievably successful in his life nevertheless. This made me doubtful about the value of an education. EM was quick to say, 'Never take me as an example. My career is an exception. I really couldn't have been anything else but a comedian.'

I didn't enjoy my schooldays. I have friends who still rant and rave about their 'wonderful days at school', but I'm not one of them. In those days, certainly, a child's enjoyment of school was very low on the agenda. I wasn't academic, I wasn't interested in the challenge of learning academic subjects, so I never came away from lessons with a warm, satisfied glow. I was one of the many who wasn't encouraged to develop a way of appreciating academic subjects, a failure of most schools at the period. Some kids have a natural aptitude, others get by through hard graft – I can see the difference in my own children. I didn't have the right attitude to apply myself to learning, and I was never taught how to.

I wasn't the only boy at Aldenham with a famous father. Arthur Lowe's son and Peter Sallis's son were my peers; Lowe was already famous as the egotistical Captain Mainwaring in *Dad's Army*, while Sallis would have to wait a while before finding fame in *Last of the Summer Wine*. I think it is fair to say that EM was on a different level of fame to those two, and I think most of the teachers at Aldenham assumed that I'd got it made just because of who my dad was. A little while ago I received a book from Aldenham, celebrating its four-hundredth anniversary, which stated with some pleasure that they had had Eric Morecambe's son at the school. They were still wallowing in it thirty years after I left! For a while I thought I was just being paranoid, but my mother made the same observation: the school thought it was a feather in its cap to have Eric Morecambe's son. EM would have been very uncomfortable with that.

Dale Winton also went to Aldenham; he's a year older than me, as I like to remind him whenever I bump into him (as I frequently do, because we share an agent, Jan Kennedy). As far as I'm aware, Dale was the first person in the school to request a transfer of boarding house because he didn't care for the décor. Dale was restless and keen to be through with school; he'd spent a nomadic childhood, presumably because of his mother's career as an actress. (An odd coincidence: Dale's mother, Sheree Winton, known as 'the English Jayne Mansfield', made a guest appearance on a Morecambe and Wise show.) I've always said it's impossible to spot talent in the young, but some people do strike you as colourful – and Dale was certainly one. If anyone at Aldenham was going to become a famous TV presenter, it was him.

Aldenham was an institution in transition when I was there. The stiff collars of a bygone era of private schools were already a thing of the past, and all around you you saw students with hair well over their collar, looking like extras from *Withnail & I*. The love-and-peace drugs-and-drop-out era was well under way; never had youth voiced its opinions so loudly. And yet Aldenham was bound by its own history and traditions – you could taste the past in every lesson, in every hall and classroom. It was a hard time to be a teacher, and it took them about ten years to get the balance right. By that time I was long gone.

One of the amendments to school protocol was the introduction of weekly boarding, which meant you could be at home for the weekend. Being a shy, home-loving lad, I don't know how I would have coped without my weekends. Every Sunday, and two 'long weekends' (Saturday and Sunday) a term, I could go home on 'exeat'. Harpenden was only half an hour's drive away, and my mother or father would pick me up after the morning chapel service at 11.30, then drop me off again at about 7pm. It was really no more than an extended Sunday lunch, but it meant the world to me. I liked it best when EM collected me, because he'd turn up in his Jensen Interceptor, and would be instantly recognized. I began to appreciate that there were some benefits to having a famous father.

I bumped into one of my old school friends in the nineties, and he was quick to remind me that when we first met I tried to impress him by explaining who my father was. 'But I hadn't heard of him, and you looked very disappointed.' I'm not sure about that; the usual reaction was one of studied disinterest.

Not everyone was so disdainful. I once had to see the school doctor, Dr Wilson, because I was suffering from stomach pains. This man never smiled, and had the nickname Dr Goebbels. 'Shirt off. Breathe in. Breathe out.' A pause. 'Your father is very funny.' Pause. 'Shirt back on. It's trapped wind. I'll give you some medicine.' Had I heard right? The exchange of glances between me and the bemused matron suggested I had. The doctor, in his own tight-lipped manner, had just confessed to being a Morecambe and Wise fan.

The school gardener was beside himself with excitement when he learned that my father was Eric Morecambe. God knows how he found out, but for a term he dogged me with questions, comments, impersonations, attempts at argument over who were the best comedians and so on. I was only thirteen; I wasn't interested in talking to him. But I felt the need, as I have always felt, to give the impression that I was interested, if only to be a good ambassador for EM. He did the same; he had to pretend to be 100 per cent committed to Morecambe and Wise whenever anyone talked to him about them. So I spent an entire term looking over my shoulder for this young, enthusiastic, slightly scary, bearded gardener, who grew more vociferous with each encounter. The relief when I heard, the following term, that he had moved on was enormous.

That sounds as if I'm whingeing. I'm not; I can assure you that a constant barrage of questions about one aspect of your

life is a serious dark cloud on your young existence. Even
now I try to avoid people who can't let the subject drop.
Someone in a village I moved to a while ago came up to me
in the street and nudged me.

'Yes?'

'It's all right,' she said. 'Your secret's safe with me.'

I had to think for a while to realize what 'secret' she was
talking about, and I moved swiftly on. With my peers at
school it was always less of a problem; they were too
absorbed in being children to be unduly concerned that I had
a famous parent. It might be brought up in a throwaway
remark: 'You're just like your Dad!' or 'You're not as funny
as your Dad.' But those moments were few and far between,
and they made little impact on my daily life.

The lecture theatre at Aldenham was a modern building,
and in the evenings the boys assembled to watch a list of
programmes that the teachers, in their infinite wisdom, had
deemed suitable viewing for testosterone-fuelled adolescents.
Morecambe and Wise fitted the bill perfectly! Watching a
recent rerun of the German PoW camp sketch in which John
Mills guest-starred, I reflected that the last time I'd seen that
show in its entirety was as a new boy at Aldenham sitting on
a solid bench in the lecture theatre with perhaps fifty other
boys, only about three of whom knew that I was Eric
Morecambe's son. I took a perverse pleasure in their
ignorance, and an enormous pride in the fact that the belly
laughs that were booming across the darkened room were all
because of EM – my father! – and my 'Uncle' Ernie.

•

Term time seemed to last forever, and the holidays were over in a flash. Home life was pretty good during this period, when I had a chance to experience it. Morecambe and Wise were bang on course again, which meant financial security for the family – this was something I cared little about at the time, but which I now realize made for a much happier, relaxed atmosphere all round. And there was a major new interest in our lives as well, since EM recovered from his heart attack: Luton Town Football Club. We were both totally besotted with the club, as EM's diaries show:

> Got up this morning – rang Luton football club to fix seats as this is my first visit for a few months. However, the kick-off was at 3 – Gary was ready, 'Fully made up' at 1.30, with his coat on! But the fog was so thick I didn't think they would play. Rang up at 2.30 and they had cancelled the match. Gary had to take his coat off! Great pity for both of us.

EM devoted his allegiance and most of his free time to the club, and during the winter months I would accompany him to as many of their home games as I could. My first visit was when EM took me to see Luton beat Oldham 4–0 in a third division match in early 1969; our last visit was just before EM's death in 1984. By that time there was hardly anyone left at the club – managers, players, personnel – who'd been there that first day. We saw the team sheet change a hundred times. Numerous managers came and went with varying degrees of success: Alan Brown, Alec Stock, Harry Haslam, David Pleat. Football was supposed to be EM's relaxation, his hobby, but it was a dangerous one for a heart-attack victim. He destroyed pipe stems with nervous bites, and his heart rate would shoot up over the ninety minutes of play. But as we can see from his diary, he may not have been the only Luton Town supporter to be affected by football in this way:

> This afternoon I went to see Luton play football. Luton 1, Walsall 0. But it was a poor game. Everybody was so kind and in the boardroom people came up and asked how I felt. One lady came up and started to talk to me about heart attacks. Her father had 3 – her husband had 4. I think she was quite pleased! But it got them both in the end. I had to laugh.

That said, he was never happier than when he was at a match. Male company, plenty of football, tea and sandwiches at half time, whisky at full time – I believe, all things considered, it was good for him. He needed a distraction, particularly in the six months after his heart attack.

When he got back to work, EM did everything he could to raise Luton's profile. He mentioned the club in jokes all the time: every opportunity was taken. Fifteen million viewers knew that he was a supporter. The finest moment was during the famous Cleopatra routine with Glenda Jackson, when EM came on holding up a Roman standard with 'Luton Town FC' boldly written across it.

By the early seventies EM had become a director of Luton Town, and he was proud of being instrumental in getting them to change their strip in 1974. They had always played in white shirts and black shorts (and have recently reverted to this strip), and, as EM used to say, 'They looked like negatives!' The new strip featured orange shirts with a black

ABOVE The house where Eric
Morecambe was born and spent
the first ten years of his life.
RIGHT Joan, a couple of years
before she met EM and at the start
of her modelling and dancing career
in 1949.
BELOW Joan and Eric shortly after their
marriage in 1952.

LEFT (left–right) Stan Stennett, Kenny Baker, Eric and Ernie, Jewell and Warriss and Tommy Cooper, 1957.

BELOW LEFT Eric and Ernie at the traditional end-of-run panto party that took place on stage the moment the audience had cleared the auditorium *c* late fifties.

BELOW Gail and Gary, aged 3 and 18 months, sitting on the doorstep of Sadie's house in Morecambe.

ABOVE EM with Joan, Gail, Gary, Ernie and Doreen Wise at Weymouth in 1961 where we had all been living in caravans for the last four months of the summer season.

TOP RIGHT The Morecambes' first house in Harpenden in 1961. Eric's dream of having his own garden finally realized.

MIDDLE RIGHT EM with Gary, Gail and his parents at their house in Hest Bank which Eric had bought them, thus fulfilling a childhood promise.

RIGHT Gary (left) and his childhood friend Bill Drysdale. Photo taken by EM who told us, 'Don't smile, just look dangerous!'

FAR RIGHT EM with his parents.

ERIC MORE

ABOVE EM and EW
rehearsing for *The
Magnificent Two*, 1964.
RIGHT EM and EW at a
read-through with
colleagues, including Sid
Green (above EM) and
Dick Hills (top) during the
Lew Grade ATV years.
RIGHT Making movies:
signing contracts with
Rank at Pinewood
Studios.
OVERLEAF The Sunshine
Boys. Eric and Ernie in
Birmingham, 1967.

and white vertical line down the front and left side, and blue shorts. They looked like a box of Liquorice Allsorts – but it was in this strip that they won promotion!

EM was always proud of Luton, whether they won or lost a match. I wanted them to win every match, and as I grew older I got more and more cynical, bemoaning the fact that they couldn't even score a goal, let alone win. EM was never like that. He went to each game with high expectations, and if things didn't go our way he just shrugged. He accepted that life had been so good to him in other ways, it would be greedy to expect to win everything.

The home supporters were proud of EM's connection with the club; away fans were less impressed, and could be quite abusive. EM took it all in good humour; it never bothered him. He would have been proud to know that, after his death, the Luton Kop, small though it is, took to chanting, 'There's only one Eric Morecambe.'

Manchester United paid a visit for a pre-season friendly – and won, unsurprisingly. George Best played, and it was a big thrill to meet him after the match. I was only about fourteen, and I was surprised that we were both about the same height. I shook hands with him, and it was like shaking hands with Liberace – all precious metal.

When we got home from a match, I'd go up to my room to replay the action on the bedroom carpet with my Subbuteo players. Subbuteo: that wonderful miniature world of plastic and cloth, and nets that never properly attached to the goal posts. On my eighteenth birthday in 1974 my parents gave me a table football set. As I write these words, I'm sitting only yards away from its tattered remains.

Beneath the dust one team still wears the strip of a long-forgotten Luton Town team.

In 1970 I had to go into hospital to have an operation on my wisdom teeth, and I was very frightened. The building was a huge Victorian edifice, and I had to have a general anaesthetic. We turned up a couple of hours before I needed to register, and so my parents took me for a walk to cheer me up, but nothing they said could allay my fears. EM, sensing my concern, said, 'It's only like Bruce Rioch having his cartilege operation. Pretend you're having the same thing.' Now, that was sound advice. Bruce Rioch – my hero, captain of Luton Town, and still in football management today – was indeed having an operation on his knee at the same time, and that gave me something to hang on to for the next few days. EM was very clever in that way; he had the ability to touch the child within himself, and so he could find just the right thing to reassure me.

EM could always zero in on the essentials of people; he was a great observer, and could sum people up in a word or a line. We went on a family visit to Portmeirion in the early seventies, when EM was fully recovered from his heart attack and was on top form.

'Look at that fella's wig! Frightening, isn't it? But he probably thinks it's wonderful.'

'You can't be sure it's a wig, Dad.'

'Get away. It's a piece of carpet. It'll have "Axminster" written down one side.'

There was only one little blip to his confidence that week, when we heard that James Beck, who played Private Walker in *Dad's Army*, had died of a heart attack at the age of thirty-

CHAPTER FIVE

nine, and that really knocked EM back. He was quiet and brooding all the following day, continually referring to it.

At home EM was full of surprises. One thing that always made Gail and me laugh was his complete hopelessness at the most mundane domestic tasks: he couldn't mend anything, or change a plug, or hang a picture, and he certainly didn't know where the tea towels lived or how to turn on the dishwasher. He wouldn't have been able to get away with it today, but Joan was always the home-maker in that relationship. When she was away, and EM had to fend for himself, things always went wrong. I came home once to find EM smirking in a very self-satisfied way; whenever he was doing that, you knew that something was going on, that something had tickled him.

'What are you up to?'

'I'm cooking chips. Want some?'

'You're cooking?' I passed.

Twenty minutes later, smoke was filling the kitchen and the hallway. The chips were burnt to a frazzle; worse still, the house could have gone up in flames. Nonchalantly he poured the charred remains into a bowl, went into the sitting room and ate the lot. I don't know what he'd have said if my mother had served up chips of that quality.

67

chapter 6

My parents built a villa in Portugal in 1965, and kept it right through to EM's death in 1984. It was an escape for them – an escape from work for EM, from the pressures of being a public figure, and for both of them a welcome escape to a simpler, more modest way of life. For us children, of course, it seemed like paradise. The sun always shone (at least in my mind's eye), and there were no distractions. We all slipped into neutral. The only headaches were the plumbing and the occasional loss of water or electricity supply, things which irritated EM so much over the years that they developed into a full-blown aversion for Portugal. 'In America,' he'd say, 'they'd get these things fixed right away. If there's a problem, it's sorted. I can't stand the third-world mentality in Portugal.' He lacked tolerance, and the occasional whiff of sewage or the odd few hours without running water would disconcert him. I suppose, in that respect, he found it hard to relax, whatever his surroundings.

When my parents started going to the Algarve, it was still described in travel brochures as 'Europe's best-kept secret' – but once that secret broke, the beauty and simplicity of the south were destroyed. It soon became a cauldron of noise and building, of packed beaches, bars and clubs – and even

English-style pubs. In the space of a single generation the slow-motion world of black-clad peasants was wiped out, and the new Portugal was hooked on the tourist economy – as if it had any choice. The young traded their ploughs for green and black Mercedes taxis.

EM did his bit to share the secret, putting his name to a magazine article entitled 'My favourite spot – it's the Algarve!', which says as much about EM as it does about Portugal.

My wife, Joan, and I built a villa just outside Albufeira in the Algarve a few years ago. Well, an Albufeira villa is a change from Aston Villa – and Luton Town, come to that!

Actually, where our villa is housed was a haven for quite a few people in show business. Cliff Richard and Frank Ifield owned villas there. Playing Des O'Connor records isn't my idea of fun – no wonder the passing bulls actually ask to go to a bullfight!

Spring and autumn are the best times of year, for I find it stifling in the summer. It's quiet then too, and we stay in the sun and save up for a trip to Albufeira and an ice cream.

At this time of year there aren't too many British holidaymakers around so I don't get recognized. Not that I mind being spotted, but it gets a bit much when I'm enjoying a spot of siesta after a drop of vinho verde only to be woken up by an autograph book prodding me in the ribs. 'Remember me? I sat in the front row when you were at Oldham in 1951. You kept looking over Ernie's shoulder and laughing at me.'

Nevertheless, the Algarve is a delightful spot for a holiday, and if you get tired of all that sea, sun and sand, there's lots of excitement in the big cities. Lisbon always conjures up memories of all those Hollywood spy films where the city was a network of espionage. I expect to see Yvonne de Carlo slinking down an alley, hotly pursued by Cesar Romero...

Then there are the picturesque markets and costumes. Rich embroidered dresses of Minho with their adornments of gold and filigree and the woollen and rough linen worsteds used in Alentego. Handicrafts are equally rich in variety, ranging from painted earthenware and crockery to quilts and wickerwork. After all this description, I think I shall have to write the next play instead of Ernie!

I'm not a bullfighting aficionado myself, but Portuguese bullfighting is unique in that the bulls are not actually killed in Portugal.

Actually, Ernie and I used to do a bullfighting routine during our music hall days. It used to get a lot of laughs...

What I find intriguing about this article is that, despite it dealing with a subject totally remote from his career, EM returns constantly to the world he knows best. There's the variety hall in Oldham, a bullfighting routine with no real relation to the article, a reference to Ernie's plays, Hollywood actors, an autograph hunter, Luton Town ... even Des O'Connor. And all this in a piece about the Algarve! Show business was his safety net. It gave him confidence, and when he had to perform as a fish out of water – writing for a magazine, for instance – it was the first place he turned for refuge.

One Portuguese summer stands out in my memory. It was 1970, EM was in fine form, fully recovered from his heart attack and ready to enjoy himself. As we boarded the Air Portugal flight at Heathrow, he broke into a loud rendition of the Beatles' 'Here Comes the Sun', much to the consternation of the other passengers, who were shuffling on in silence. He had no sense of embarrassment, and thought it funny when other people did. The more I said, 'Be quiet, Dad!', the louder he sang. EM could be very direct and unabashed. This, after all, is the man whose way of teaching me the facts of life was to drop his trousers and say, 'These can be dangerous things, son.' ·

When we arrived in the Algarve, people kept coming up to EM and asking, 'Are you feeling better, then?' He had to think for a moment before he realized that people were still concerned about his heart attack two years before.

The villa in Portugal was practical, not lavish. It had whitewashed walls and brown varnished shutters reminding me of the cover of the Graham Greene novel *Our Man in Havana*. Our ears reverberated to the chirp of crickets, and our nostrils were full of the overwhelming scent of the almond trees that speckled the sloping land at the rear of the property. There wasn't a sign of any grass, and anything that flowered had long since been burnt out. EM stood at the edge of the property and swung his hand in a vague southerly direction. 'Von day, my son, all diss vill be yours...' The accent was hard to pinpoint; there was a hint of Mexican. (And one day all this would not be mine: after EM's death my mother decided the place was giving her too much hassle, and rightly sold it.)

The main drawback of going on holiday with EM was that he couldn't swim and didn't like sand – therefore he wasn't very involved in the experience of a family holiday. When he did wander down to the shoreline – invariably wearing long trousers – he wouldn't stick around too long. He'd give the ocean and the sand a wary glance, dip a toe in the surf, and then take himself off for a walk. He'd find an alcove or a sheltered spot on the cliff top, and sit down and smoke his pipe. Back at the villa he'd sit on the patio in the shade of an overhanging bamboo, quietly tinkering around with ideas for *The Morecambe and Wise Show*, a glass of shandy on the table in front of his portable typewriter, while the rest of us played on the beach. He was quite content with his solitude – it was a refreshing break from the frenetic pace of his working life. In fact, most of his leisure pursuits – fishing, photography, birdwatching, painting – were solitary. He really did enjoy his own company, time away from the animated conversation and quips, a retreat into his own shell.

It would have been nice if he'd joined us more, and I think EM missed out on a great deal of pleasure by not being able to swim. His parents should have made him take swimming lessons, but he was put off for life when some bright spark pushed him into the deep end at the local baths. Yet, if he'd spent his time with us in the sea, we might never have seen the Tom Jones or Shirley Bassey routines on the show; EM had the idea for both of these during his solitary hours on the patio.

Not that EM was always quiet on holiday; far from it. He spent a great deal of time gagging, to the point when it could become quite irritating. One day he got hold of a false moustache which gave him hours of fun. He loved little props like that; at one point he took to wearing a funny hat and walking with a limp, delighted with the idea that this would prevent people from recognizing him. Most of the time we enjoyed EM's gags as much as he did, but the endless assault of mischief could be tiring. Watching a favourite programme that he had decided to interrupt, or reading a book, was impossible. You couldn't be angry with him, because it would change nothing. We just applied forbearance.

When I tell interviewers that living with EM was like living with a watered-down version of *The Morecambe and Wise Show*, they don't always believe me, but it's true. They can't believe he was really like that – but what you saw on TV was, in essence, him. Yes, he was giving a performance when he was working, but it was a performance built entirely round his own character. His success was largely due to the public's recognition that they were watching a real person. His alter ego was only a very minor modification of his real self. So his family lived in this twilight world of Morecambe and Wise. There were none of the face slaps or the wiggling glasses at home – these were bits of business, the tools of his trade, as he called them – but in other respects it was like living with a full-time comedian. That's what EM was, and he could never stop.

The only gag that he was always doing at home was his perennial Long John Silver impersonation. He 'did' Silver in a sketch with Arthur Lowe, and in the Antony and Cleopatra sketch with Glenda Jackson; he'd grab his right leg and hide it, and he was off. I don't think he was obsessed with *Treasure Island* – he just saw great comic possibilities in Long John Silver, with the parrot, the peg leg, the Zumerzet accent. Even in my early childhood I can remember him walking around the house clutching one leg and saying, 'Aarrrr, Jim lad, do ye be wantin' this cup o' tea? It'll warm the cockles.' It stayed with him all his life; the desire to perform spontaneous Long John Silver impersonations never left him, like some colourful ghost haunting him from past pantomine seasons.

Our neighbour in Portugal was Muriel Young, the children's television presenter (remember Ollie Beak?), who, by 1970, was the head of children's programmes at Granada. Mu and her husband Cyril were an important part of our life in Portugal, not least because Mu was the only one of us who had bothered to learn enough Portuguese to be able to communicate with the maid. And they were great entertainers, which EM and Joan were not, so they became the focus of much of our social life there. Mu loved entertaining; she'd arrive on the flight from London at lunchtime, nip to the local shops and rustle up a dinner party for twelve, fourteen, even sixteen people by 8 p.m. She invariably invited a curious mix of characters. Ex-RAF types would sit opposite out-and-out communists. An author, whose name I forget but who bore a remarkable resemblance to Quentin Crisp, sat opposite a landowner, a German the right age to have done his bit in repelling the allies during the Second World War sat next to ... well, Eric Morecambe, or Cilla Black, or Tom Jones, or Marc Bolan. Muriel knew everyone, and she loved to mix them all up together. I wish I'd been old enough to appreciate those dinners at the time, and not just in retrospect.

I was delighted to run into Muriel Young years later, in 1999, at the launch of a book of anecdotes about EM that I'd written with Martin Sterling, *Memories of Eric*, to which Mu had contributed a tale or two. She reminded me how, as a boy, I had a habit of finishing EM's stories, which used to drive him mad. He'd be approaching the punchline, then I would casually intercept and say it for him. No malice intended – it just came from years of hearing the same stories. This happened once back at home, when we were visiting Uncle Alan's pub in north London, and I butted in with a punchline. EM was livid. Alan defused the atmosphere with a laugh, but EM was not amused. He was not looking for a double-act with his son.

EM continued to go to Portugal for the rest of his life, enjoying it a little less with every visit. The development of Albufeira spoilt things for us. When we first started going, the road which ran parallel to ours was little more than a dirt track; we could drive down it, just, without coming across a single car. You'd often get stuck in a sand-trap, and have to dig yourself out with a shovel. Ten years later the road was tarred and lined with discos, clubs, bars and neon signs, a round-the-clock cacophony, and it just wasn't the same. EM started calling it 'Portugal's equivalent of Blackpool's Golden Mile', but eventually he lost his sense of humour about it. There were some advantages to the growth of tourism in the Algarve. The roads were better, there were supermarkets and banks within easy reach – but the rustic charm of Albufeira that had drawn them there in the first place was gone for ever.

One unexpected result of the influx of Brits to the Algarve became apparent when we were walking down a back street in Albufeira one day and found ourselves pursued by waving arms and smiles from the local people. EM was flattered but nonplussed – until we turned a corner and saw, outside the local fleapit, a large colour photo of Morecambe and Wise.

They were showing *The Magnificent Two* – and what the Portuguese made of it we couldn't imagine. The irony of travelling all the way from Hertfordshire to find that one of his own films was doing a two-week run in Portugal tickled EM.

chapter 7

I loved being in EM's company when I was young, but I had
to be in the right mood. Perhaps I was too sensitive, and
perhaps EM was inconsiderate at times. I remember walking
with him down a hot dusty track somewhere abroad,
probably Portugal, when I was about twelve. I pulled up
abruptly by a giant ant hill – a pyramid created from billions
of grains of dirt that must have looked way bigger than the
pyramids of Giza to the worker ants painstakingly
transporting each grain. The magic of nature overwhelmed
me, and I called out to EM, who was a few steps behind me,
'Look at this!' He came over and nodded. 'Oh yes. They
never give up. They won't give up till the job's finished.' And
with that, he kicked the pyramid down, sending the ants into
complete confusion. To say I was livid would be putting it
mildly; I hated my father more at that moment than I'd ever
hated anyone. I should have told him, but instead I stifled it –
the usual reaction of a boy brought up in the stiff-upper-lip
environment of private education.

The anger subsided as the day passed. We went to the
beach and returned along the same track. I'd almost
forgotten about the destroyed ant hill. 'Look!' called EM,
and I strolled over. The pyramid was complete again. 'I told

you,' he said softly. 'They never give up. It's a good lesson.'

On my fourteenth birthday, he took me for lunch in the revolving restaurant on top of London's GPO Tower, as it was then called. He insisted on smoking his pipe in the lift, which really irritated me, and as a joke he blew smoke in my face just as I was inhaling. I thought I was going to choke to death. EM, of course, told me not to make such a fuss, and just wanted to laugh the whole thing off. But children aren't good at laughing things off; if I did that sort of thing to one of my own kids, they'd give me a mouthful of abuse. That wasn't the way back then, at least not in the Morecambe family, and so that minor incident grated beyond all reason, and for the next hour I truly hated my father. In the bigger picture it meant nothing, but the anger was genuine enough at the time. It didn't spoil my day; after lunch we went to the Odeon in Leicester Square to see *Oliver!*, which remains one of my favourite films – just as the day remains one of my happiest birthdays.

Our family was completed in 1973, when EM and Joan adopted my brother Steven, then aged three. Gail was working at a nursery nursing college and would occasionally bring various unfortunate children home on visits. Steven was a foster child looking for an adoptive family, and within weeks of his first summer visits he was calling my mother 'Mum'. Gail understood his tough background better than anyone, and when she asked EM and Joan if they'd consider adopting him, the idea was not unacceptable. EM's attitude was that it was up to Joan to make the decision; she was the one who'd have to deal with all the day-to-day problems and work associated with having a small child in the house.

Gail and I are separated by two and a half years; Steven and I by fourteen. When he arrived, I was on the way to becoming an adult, so there were no sibling rivalry difficulties. I felt fatherly towards him more than brotherly, and today he tells me that he has always seen me more as a father than a brother. He lost EM when he was fourteen, so that's understandable.

I left Aldenham School in 1973, so little Steven was a very good companion during the empty time between school and college – someone to take for a walk and buy ice creams. When I lost my voice one day, we found Steven poking around in the garden.

'What are you doing?'

'Gary's lost his voice. I'm trying to find it.'

He was instantly, and fully, embraced as a member of the Morecambe family. None of us ever made him feel that he was an interloper who struck lucky. I suppose if you chose to analyse the situation in that way, that's what he was – but that's not the way we play the game in our family. You're either in or out, and Steven's in. It's as simple as that.

Steven remembers those early visits to our house; he even remembers the adoption home, because his feet used to stick out of the end of the bed. Gail would bring him over in her car, and he was supposed to sleep during the drive, but was always too excited to do so. In the summer he'd bob around in the pool in his armbands; it must have made a wonderful contrast to the adoption home, so it's little wonder that he started to think of our home as his home. He'd latched on to Gail from the very start, and because he heard her calling EM and Joan Mum and Dad, he started to do the same.

Steven went to school, and eventually moved up to Sibford School in Oxfordshire – another boarding school. The bullying started on his first day, the moment EM and Joan drove off down the drive – all because EM was famous. Someone poured scalding hot tea down his neck, and for the next two years it was sheer hell – until he was big enough to fight back. But to start with, Steven was terribly homesick. Mum would load him up with tuck to take back to school, little realizing that it would all be nicked the moment he arrived.

Steven remembers EM as being much sterner than I do. Steven's language, at the time of his adoption, was appalling – he knew all the swear words before he knew any others. EM would tell him off, and Steven would dart out to the kitchen to take refuge with Joan, hiding behind her while EM tried to get at him. Joan would tell EM to go off and calm down, while Steven laughed or stuck his tongue out, which was not the sort of behaviour that EM would have appreciated at all. But EM would get his own back; he never forgot. Long after Steven had forgotten all about it, EM would give him a little flick or a pinch and say, 'That was for earlier!'

•

As I grew into my teens, I became more conscious of friction between EM and me – or at least I became conscious of some of his shortcomings as a father. He could encourage you one minute, then knock you right back the next – just as when he heard Gail playing the piano, then knocked spots off her with his own improvisation. He'd take Steven fishing, and get very excited if Steven hooked a big one, but then if he lost it he'd tell him off for disappointing him, and for over-reacting if he was upset. When I was in my early teens, I got very into model aircraft, and I'd spend hours assembling and painting them from plastic kits. EM was impressed, but he recognized that I was a messy model-maker and that he could do better; the daubs of paint and blobs of glue all over the place distressed him. 'You make beautiful model planes,' he said, 'it's just that we could do without the house being redecorated each time.'

EM was a superb model-maker. I don't know where that talent sprang from, because Airfix kits weren't around when he was a lad, but he was really good. I had a De Havilland Comet 4B set, which had to be painted in the full BEA livery of bright red wings, and I knew I couldn't do it without getting red paint everywhere. EM said he'd help, and he spent an entire Sunday morning poring over dozens of grey plastic parts and pots of paint. He used sticky tape to protect the flaps from being painted red instead of silver; very serious stuff, model-making.

When he'd finished, he brought the Comet into my bedroom. 'There you go, son. Just don't play with it until the paint has fully dried.'

'But it is dry!' I protested.

'No, it just looks dry. Give it an hour.'

'Okay, Dad. I'll give it an hour.'

Did I hell. Ten minutes later the plane was in my hands, and so was the sticky paint, which smudged all along the fuselage. 'Time for repairs,' I thought anxiously, and started touching it up with a brush. Within fifteen minutes all EM's hard work was undone. The plane was ruined.

'How does it look?' asked EM the next day.

'What?'

'The Comet I made for you. How does it look?'

'Fine. It looks fine.' My heart was thumping.

'Good.'

A plan grew in my head. 'Dad?'

'Yes?'

'It would be better if I had another one to go with it.'

'What do you need another one for?'

'It will be more realistic, like a real airport. You never see just one of them at an airport...'

'Okay, but it'll be the last one I make for you.'

Phew!

Whenever EM was planted on the drawing-room sofa puffing a pipe, I would quickly find one of my planes and rush in to use the smoke as clouds. He was surprisingly tolerant of this, although there was a limit to how much 'strato-cumulus' he could create before going green. I think he reacted positively to genuine enthusiasm. He overwhelmed me once by making a tape recording of the vacuum cleaner that, if lifted, sounded just like a plane taking off. He recorded about fifteen minutes of this, and I can picture him standing with the microphone over the cleaner, trying to time the plane's taxiing, charge down the runway and take-off to perfection. He then took me and the cassette down to his car and left me to play. I used the steering wheel and the controls as my flight deck, and it gave me hours of pleasure.

My love of model aircraft didn't last, though. EM returned from the studios one summer afternoon, and as usual I was playing airports in the garden. EM climbed out of his Rolls-Royce, took one look at me and said, 'I wish I could spend all day just pretending to fly aeroplanes.'

That was it. I never picked up a toy plane again.

He didn't mean to put me off; it was just a throwaway remark from a tired man who had spent a long hot day at the TV studios. In fact, years later I brought the subject up again. 'Did I really put you off when I said that?' he asked me, aghast at the thought.

'It's okay,' I replied. 'I needed to move on. You just triggered a reaction that was due at any moment.' He seeemd happier about that.

When he was in the right frame of mind, EM loved to play. He was brilliant at origami, and could make a vast range of paper darts with wavering tail fins, some 6 inches long, that would make the dart spin, when launched, in gentle circles.

It wasn't just in the little things that EM displayed this odd mixture of encouragement and knocking-back. He had the same strange attitude to our developing ambitions, as Gail and I moved into young adulthood. Gail had some interest in becoming a model, and had met an art director who was interested in helping her to put together a portfolio. When he called to arrange a time for her to go to her first photo-shoot, Gail asked her parents' permission. They both said, 'You must do what you want to do, darling,' but the look on their faces said that they thought it was a really bad idea. By the time Gail got back to the phone, she'd decided that she didn't want to be a model after all. Partly this was just EM's understandable distrust of the business; he'd been in show business for long enough to know that there's a sordid side to it, as well as a lot of disappointment. He'd have wanted Gail to be exceptionally good if she went into modelling, and would have been embarrassed if she'd been less than great. When it came to any aspect of performing, EM was a perfectionist.

When I was sixteen, I'd made up my mind that I wanted to be a writer. I tried my hand during my last year at school with various ludicrously extended essays, which I'd bring home on exeat and read to EM. He was fascinated by my interest in writing, and would always say something encouraging, like, 'Just keep at it. It's never easy.' Then I'd read him poems I'd written, and he'd nod and say, 'Great. But don't write too many too quickly. You'll end up like Ernie and the plays wot he writes.'

When I left school, I tried to write a children's book with my friend Bill Drysdale, who was a dab hand at illustrations. We were both enamoured of fantasy fiction, especially *The Lord of the Rings*, and I showed EM our first effort.

'It's very good,' he said.

'Not bad considering our age.'

'A publisher won't judge it by your age, only by whether or not it's publishable.'

I got much better advice from Dennis Holman, who had been commissioned to ghost-write the first Morecambe and Wise biography, *Eric and Ernie*. He told me that I needed to write at least a quarter of a million words and throw them away, just for the experience, to learn how to play around with characters and ideas and narrative. He was right: suddenly I wasn't writing with the fear of rejection hanging over me. Instead, I was learning my trade, and I left school with the definite idea of becoming a writer in my mind. There was, however, a long way to go before I got there.

chapter 8

During the school holidays I was lucky enough to be allowed to go to the studios to watch *The Morecambe and Wise Show* being filmed. Usually I'd take a friend with me – Bill Drysdale, my best friend from home, or Nick Kerr and Steve Fountaine from school.

Filming is the most boring process imaginable if you're not directly involved – and even if you are, it's tedious at best. There's so much hanging around in between takes, and nothing is shot in any kind of order, so it makes sense only when it's all put together and screened. But at least I was witness to something that is now entertainment history: I can watch them putting the boot on Shirley Bassey's foot, or singing backing vocals for Tom Jones, or playing the piano with André Previn, and I can honestly say that I was there at the time. The Previn (Preview, Previtt) sketch is probably my favourite Morecambe and Wise moment; Victoria Wood reckons it's the greatest comedy sketch of all time. Apparently André Previn's son didn't see the sketch until he was about thirty, and immediately phoned his father and said, 'Dad! I didn't realize you could be so funny!'

EM could get a laugh just by walking on stage, and there's not many comedians who can do that. Tommy Cooper could;

I can't think of anyone else. I must have seen Eric and Ernie performing over a hundred times, and on each occasion you could hear the chuckling start up the moment EM appeared. Ernie would come on first, and launch into one of his spiels, there was a three-second pause, and then on came EM. 'Evening, all. Enjoying yourself?' It always got a laugh – but EM wasn't trying to be funny. He just was. And that is a gift that no amount of planning and experience and solid hard work can give you.

In between rehearsals and takes, there was chat. Ernie was always very welcoming; he'd fire loads of questions at me and my guests, keen to know what we were doing at school and what interested us. EM wasn't so interested in schoolwork; he wanted to know what TV programmes we liked, what my friends thought of Morecambe and Wise, whether they'd ever been to a TV studio before. He gagged around between takes, trying to make us laugh, which he invariably did; it was important for him to keep buoyed up, even when nothing was happening.

There's a much-repeated anecdote about EM and the one-armed commissionaire at the BBC, which goes like this:

Commissionaire: Hello, Eric. How about a ticket to see your show?
EM: Sorry, I can't do that.
Commissionaire (disappointed): Oh, why not?
EM: You can't clap.

Alan Bennett recalls the story in his diary *Writing Home*, with some suggestion that it's apocryphal – but I can authenticate it, because I was standing next to EM at the time. And the commissionaire fell about laughing. EM always knew how far he could go without giving offence. I've read that Groucho Marx was the same, and I can often see a lot of Groucho in EM's performance.

It's ironic that EM was no joke teller. His gift was the ability to find humour in people's comments and everyday situations. I can only recall one occasion when he told me a joke. It sticks in my mind, not so much because of the joke, as I never remember jokes, but because of the uniqueness of the event:

'Have you seen Stevie Wonder's new car?'

'No.' I answered dutifully.

'Well, neither has he!'

And that was the joke. The only joke. Ever.

As the *The Morecambe and Wise Show* gathered steam on BBC1, guest stars started to become more and more important; it's what Eric and Ernie became most famous for. The best guest stars were 'straight' personalities; it never worked so well when they had other comedians. The point was proved when they had Leonard Rossiter on the show. He was great in an Andrews Sisters sketch with Eric and Ernie, but in the front-of-tabs routine just prior to it the script had been developed to give him the best lines, and it just didn't work. The audience wanted to see Eric and Ernie, particularly Eric, getting the best lines, and getting the better of their guest. EM knew that it hadn't worked, that they'd deviated from a successful formula, but he loved Leonard Rossiter, who was a family friend, and wanted him to get the laughs.

Another guest star who didn't work out was Harold Wilson, who was neither actor nor musician nor comedian, but a real live politician. If you watch that routine now, you can see Eric and Ernie working their balls off to keep it moving. Harold Wilson was very funny when he made speeches or talked to the press, but as a performer his timing was imperfect, to say the least. You can see Eric playing around in the background using every tiny bit of experience from forty years to make that sketch happen. They just about got away with it, and after the show EM said to me, 'It was great. Very unusual, but it worked.' Only just.

What people responded to in these sketches was the humanizing of the guest star. In the sixties and seventies it was rare to see a well-known person stepping outside what they were principally known for; there was a great deal more mystique surrounding famous people than there is now, and I think *The Morecambe and Wise Show* was partly responsible for breaking it down and revealing that these people were ordinary and funny after all. The classic example, of course, is when Angela Rippon, the very elegant newsreader, stepped out from behind her desk and flashed those fantastic legs in a dance routine. We all loved the way in which these people were taken down from their pedestals – but, because it was Morecambe and Wise, we knew that it would be done in a friendly, funny way that would give us, the viewers, a human connection with those figures. Rather than being humiliated, the guest stars were celebrated and in a sense elevated, even though, like Shirley Bassey with her boot, they'd had to undergo some pretty humiliating treatment. The stars cottoned on quickly; appearing on *The Morecambe and Wise*

Show inspired a kind of collective love, a bonding process which has proved to be very enduring. Whatever you may think of someone, once you realize that they've got a sense of humour and are willing to laugh at themselves, it's hard not to warm to them.

The Angela Rippon routine was on the 1976 Christmas show, and you always knew that a Morecambe and Wise Christmas show would have really good guests in the big number. People have come to define their Christmases, and their family history, by these shows: 'I remember seeing the newsreaders singing "There is Nothing Like a Dame"' – that kind of thing. The Christmas shows are still regarded as a high water mark in British television, and rightly so. Nothing else has ever brought the nation together in quite the same way.

But that kind of success brought its own problems. EM became very tense in the few days leading up to the recording of a Christmas special. Usually he was fine when he was working, but Christmas was different – that was the time to avoid any kind of confrontation with him, even something as simple as 'Good morning, Dad!' So many months of preparation went into that hour of airtime, it's little wonder he got uptight. It was all very well to know that the material was good – he actually had to go out there and make sure that it was *the* event of the Christmas season. It was a big responsibility, and one that he felt more and more with every year. Questions like 'Do you make it up as you go along?' didn't make life any easier – and that was asked on many an occasion. Someone once said, 'You're like a vicar; you only work on Sundays.' EM just bit his lip.

Once the show was out of the way, you could feel the

tension lifting, and EM was like a lamb. It was over and done, and he knew it was great. He didn't even get tense when the show was about to go out on television; in fact, he never referred to it until about fifteen minutes before transmission, and then it was just to make sure we all knew which room we were going to be sitting in so there wouldn't be a last-minute kerfuffle.

Sometimes I tried to help EM during the run-up to a show. On one occasion in the early seventies he was learning a script, walking round and round the back garden saying his lines and doing the actions, looking completely insane. He asked me to do Ernie's part – it was one of the plays wot Ernie wrote, set in the 1920s, which starred long-suffering guest Michelle Dotrice. I made such a pig's ear of the rehearsal that EM gently took the script off me.

'I'll manage on my own, thank you.'

'I can do it, Dad. Really I can.'

'Yes, yes. You go and have a lie-down.'

My only concrete contribution to *The Morecambe and Wise Show* came when EM was going through a musical number that involved Latin American dancing with Vanessa Redgrave. I said to him, 'When you have the violin playing, why can't another instrument be heard instead?' He said, 'That's a good idea,' but he didn't sound exactly overwhelmed. Then on the 1973 Christmas show, there it is, with a little bit of Morecambe and Wise embellishment. It is Ernie, I think, who goes to play the violin, but we hear a trumpet. Eric starts signalling frantically to his partner, who then turns the violin around and starts blowing into the end. A minor moment, but a great personal memory.

Christmas, as far as EM was concerned, was about the family gathering. He genuinely enjoyed that. I remember sitting down with him one Christmas morning to watch a Laurel and Hardy film; he was almost choked with emotion. 'Just sit back and admire true genius at work,' he said. All of his favourite comics – Laurel and Hardy, the Marx Brothers, Abbott and Costello, Phil Silvers, Jack Benny – came to affect him more and more emotionally. They made him feel better about the world he lived in, and that's exactly what EM did for millions of his own fans. He had no pretensions about his comedy, and he never minded if people didn't like him. 'You can't please all the people all of the time,' he'd say. 'The most you can hope for is that you make some of the people laugh some of the time.' EM's comedy was all about the imperfections and disappointments of life; he made those things funny, and so he made us feel better about them. It was all part of the humanizing process of Morecambe and Wise's comedy. EM himself didn't analyse it. The nearest he came in my hearing to making any comment on this aspect of his work was: 'Life's not Hollywood. It's Cricklewood.'

Morecambe and Wise had been greatly influenced by other double acts before them, notably Laurel and Hardy, Abbott and Costello, Flanagan and Allen and Jewel and Warriss. Jimmy Jewel and Ben Warriss were once introduced by Ed Sullivan on American TV as 'Jewels and his Walrus'; Eric and Ernie fared little better, as he introduced them as a triple act: 'Morey, Camby and Wise'.

In their turn Morecambe and Wise were a huge influence on the double acts that came after them; it's impossible now for any male double act to avoid comparisons to Morecambe

and Wise. Reeves and Mortimer get it all the time, and so do
Ant and Dec – and they're all great fans of Eric and Ernie.

Recently I've noticed that Vic Reeves has become a little
dismissive of comparisons to Eric Morecambe, and I can
understand this: it must hang around his neck like a millstone
at times. But then he has brought this upon himself. While
having a similar look to EM that I'm sure is natural, his
mannerisms and style of delivery have visibly been honed on EM.

Ant and Dec have also styled themselves on Eric and
Ernie, but less consciously I would say. 'I think it makes good
journalism as much as anything else,' Ant told me. 'Two
people together and it becomes "Oh, well you must have
been influenced by Morecambe and Wise." But don't get me
wrong – we're huge fans.'

'We did a flat routine for a while, which was much more a
deliberate homage to Eric and Ernie,' said Dec. 'Actually,
we've always been hugely flattered by the comparison.'

Eric and Ernie's closest peers in the seventies were Mike
and Bernie Winters, two brothers touring theatres and
making TV shows in exactly the same way as Morecambe
and Wise. When interviewed by BBC radio once, EM was
asked by a rather pompous presenter what he and Ernie
would have been if they hadn't become comics. Without
missing a beat, EM replied, 'Mike and Bernie Winters.'

Mike and Bernie Winters were trapped by the standard
format of previous double acts – the idiot and the know-all.
Eric and Ernie had started there as well, but thanks to Eddie
Braben, the writer of all their BBC shows, they progressed
way beyond it, redefining the art of the double act, blurring
the edges so much that it was sometimes hard to tell who was

PREVIOUS PAGE Just prior to his first heart
attack, and the strain is beginning to show.
ABOVE EM with Joan, Gary and Ernie,
switching on the illuminations c1969.
RIGHT Comedians, yes ... male models, no.

ABOVE Eric in Australia. Taking time out from saving the duo's flagging fortunes.
LEFT The condemned man – Gary's last day of freedom before boarding school, September 1969.

LEFT In rehearsal with Ann Hamilton. EM is sporting his favourite jumper and ever-present collar and tie.
ABOVE Eric with Joan, trying to get Barney the dog to pose for the camera, c1971.
BELOW Contrived domesticity – EM with his parents at home, the only time you'll ever see him in the kitchen, c1970.

TOP QE2 cruise, Easter 1971.
ABOVE LEFT EM demonstrating how to dive, despite not being able to swim!
ABOVE RIGHT Eric's son Steven, aged 8.

ABOVE EM, Liberace, Joan's mum Alice, and Joan. EM had arranged this meeting especially for Joan, a life-long fan of the great Liberace.
OVERLEAF EM in contemplative mood during rehersals in 1972.

the straight man and who was the clown. Look at any of their great routines, like my favourite with André Previn, and it's possible to see that the sketch could have been rewritten to switch the roles. Eric could have been the MC, Ernie the pianist. It might not have worked so well, but it would have been possible. Eric and Ernie were very flexible performers. I've heard it said that certain other double acts would always call for a retake if they made a mistake; Eric and Ernie enjoyed those little slips and made them part of the act.

It always surprised EM that there was so little competition around during the seventies; I think they would have enjoyed the challenge. The competition, when it came, did not look likely to trouble them: Little and Large, and Cannon and Ball.

One evening Ernie phoned EM to ask if he'd seen *The Little and Large Show* that evening. 'Yes,' replied EM, 'I don't think we've got much to worry about, do you?' In fairness to Little and Large, they never tried to usurp Morecambe and Wise. They simply took advantage of opportunities, and you can't blame them for that. At best I found them unimpressive, at worst appalling; Eddie Large is a reasonable mimic, but Sid Little was never a reasonable comic. But they kept on going, and you have to admire that kind of inexhaustible self-belief.

Cannon and Ball were much more promising. They had sparkle and understanding, and a history that bonded them long before they stepped in front of a camera. They were both strong, confident performers, and EM thought they had real potential, and was disappointed that they never got beyond their own starting point. He also liked them as people, and was flatttered when Bobby Ball described EM in his autobiography as 'our hero'. But Cannon and Ball got stuck in a rut. Their early stuff, 'Rock on, Tommy!' and the stretching of Bobby's braces, worked fine for about five years, but they never evolved. Eventually their act faded through the crumbling of their relationship. By the time they'd resolved that, the public had moved on. Eric and Ernie never fell out; a large part of their success was due to the fact that they stayed together, and they became a single entity in the minds of the public.

EM had a curious attitude to his showbiz peers. He wasn't a great one for celebrity parties; unlike Muriel Young, he didn't fill his house with all the stars that he met, and he met plenty. But he enjoyed the company of fellow professionals, even when he was supposed to be escaping from all that. If someone famous arrived in Portugal, for instance, he was always keen to see them. On one occasion, my friend Bill and I thought we'd seen Roger Moore in a bar, and we told Eric. His eyes lit up. 'Roger's here? Where?' He'd known Roger Moore since the fifties, when Moore was modelling pullovers and EM was doing radio guest spots. He was so disappointed when the gentleman in question turned out not to be Roger Moore – and, in fact, looked nothing like him. What intrigued me was how much EM wanted it to be Roger Moore. He wanted that show-business camaraderie, even though he was on holiday. It was in his blood.

Equally, EM could be cruel to other celebrities without even realizing it. I've often wondered about the real nature of his relationship with Des O'Connor, who was the butt of endless EM jokes. Des, Eric and Ernie met in the early fifties, when they'd drive around together between various gigs. Des was only doing comedy then, but he announced to EM that he wanted to be a singer as well. EM was so amused by this that he would constantly tease Des about it – but it wasn't until *The Morecambe and Wise Christmas Show* of 1972 that he brought it up in front of millions. Des was uncomfortable with that gag. He had friends, family and fans to think about, and the family – particularly the daughters at school – suffered badly because of the insults. My mother says that EM would have stopped the gags immediately if he'd known that he was hurting anyone – but he didn't know, and the gag continued. Des has undeniably done very well from it, and acknowledges the fact himself. One of his daughters said, in an interview, that it's better to be looked over than overlooked, so perhaps no harm was done after all, long term at least.

I met Des O'Connor in the later seventies, when I was working for Billy Marsh, Morecambe and Wise's agent. Des came in for a meeting, and Billy called me into his office.

'Des,' said Billy, 'I'd like you to meet Gary.' Des half stood and shook my hand, while I smiled and waited for the punchline.

'Gary works for me.'

'I see,' said Des, not seeing at all, his mouth set in a grin.

'And his father is Eric Morecambe.'

The penny dropped. Des leapt to his full height – all four foot two – and grabbed me round the throat. 'The years of anguish I've suffered because of your father!' he began, and then burst out laughing.

EM really liked Des – and his music. When Des appeared on a Morecambe and Wise Christmas show and sang *Feelings*,

EM turned to me and said, without irony or a gag in sight, 'That's one of the best numbers I've ever heard Des sing.'

And normally EM *would* rather make a gag. As writer and producer John Fisher once told me, 'The thing with Morecambe, Milligan and Marx is that they *thought* funny.'

Rolf Harris tells a story in his autobiography *Can You Tell What It Is Yet?*, which sums up this aspect of EM very accurately:

> The moment Eric saw me he said, 'Hello, sunshine.' Then he launched into a series of clever jokes about Australians that had everyone laughing. I couldn't think of a thing to say. I can't remember a single one of the jokes now, but they were all very clever put-downs. I think Eric was expecting me to come back with as good as I got, but I couldn't compete. I was swamped and went under, looking red-faced and miserable. I don't think he was being malicious. He simply knew what buttons to press to make people laugh.

chapter 9

I left school in 1973 with little idea of what I wanted to do with the rest of my life other than a vague idea that I'd like to be a writer. By this time Morecambe and Wise were approaching the height of their career, and the pressure was getting to EM; he could, at times, be snappy. My mother blamed the whisky, with which EM liked to relax over dinner – but it didn't relax him, it changed his character and made him aggressive. I'm the same.

Over dinner one day a friend of the family asked me what plans I had for the future, which was unfortunate as my plans were excessively slight at the time. 'Well,' I replied, 'we've been looking at journalism as an idea.' 'We' was my mother and I; she'd been helping me find out about various possible careers. EM flew off the handle. 'We!' he said loudly. 'It should be you!' My mother calmed him down, our friends kept quiet, and I squirmed with embarrassment. I should have seen it coming; all of us in the family knew how to read the signs, and we could tell when EM was feeling volatile. You'd see him grimace with anger or irritation when approached by fans, yet he'd give them the impression that he was jovial, happy, relaxed.

It was important to EM that his children stood on their

own two feet, and yet he was far from encouraging about the careers we chose to follow. I don't think he could ever fully enter into these considerations; he was so wrapped up in his own career that it was very hard for him to think much about his children's. What mattered to EM was that he'd worked his way up from nothing and, thanks to talent and a great deal of hard graft, he'd succeeded. He wanted us to do the same, I suppose, but the circumstances were different. Gail, Steven and I grew up in an environment where there was never any shortage of money; there wasn't the same incentive to get out there and fight, because our nest was very comfortably feathered. And although we were lucky to have all the contacts that anyone could possibly desire, there was very little encouragement from EM to pursue any of those opportunities. I suppose, in retrospect, I was no different from thousands of other teenage kids from affluent homes who don't 'need' to go out to work; I had a vague idea that I might be able to do something, but I didn't know what, and there was no great sense of urgency about finding out.

There were times, though, when EM adopted a very hands-on approach to being a father. I took the summer of 1975 out to travel around Europe with my friends Bill Drysdale and Phil Watkins; it was the era of the Inter Rail ticket, a cheap way of getting happy young backpackers to travel on the continent. Just before our departure, EM called me into his bedroom.

'Now, you'll take plenty of condoms, won't you?' he asked seriously.

I laughed. 'Dad, this is a hike across Europe, not an orgy!'

'Well, you never know. It's better to be safe than sorry.'

It reminded me of another of EM's favourite pieces of advice on the subject of sex: 'It's better to be hot and frustrated, than satisfied and worried.'

A part of EM felt that he was saying goodbye to his son for good; he had some idea that backpacking in Europe was dangerous, and that a call would come through three weeks later to tell him that my partially buried body had been found just outside Paris or Milan or Rome. Therefore, when he saw three starved male figures approaching his villa in Portugal later that summer, he was rather pleased. He acted as if our visit were a spontaneous one: 'Wa-hey! The boys are here!' He ran indoors, reappearing with a camera to record the moment. An hour or two later, the actor Tim Brooke-Taylor turned up at the villa. 'Tim,' said EM, 'the boys are here!' Tim told me later that he thought the local mafia had turned up.

EM enjoyed Bill Drysdale's company, and Bill enjoyed EM's. They'd known each other since Bill and I were four years old, and they hit it off instantly. Bill was a good straight man for EM, possibly without ever realizing it. Unlike with his own family, EM could mess about with Bill verbally without getting bored retorts or moody silences. Not that I was like that much of the time, but you know what families are like – familiarity breeds contempt. However, someone who turns up regularly at the house, like extended family, gives rise to fresh opportunities – and EM was quick to pounce.

Bill's a very easy-going bloke, and he was much more academically inclined than I was. After school Bill was heading for an exam that would lead him to Oxford

University, while I was heading nowhere in particular. I took my driving test and passed first time – and so I should have done, because I had nothing else to distract me. I briefly flirted with the idea of becoming a driving instructor, but dropped that soon enough: within two months I'd written off one car and damaged another. EM was incensed about the first crash, sympathetic about the second. This was nothing to do with the circumstances of either accident; it was just that his mood coloured his reaction to any situation.

EM was not the best of fathers to have around when you were a teenager with bewildering ideas and emotions. The thought of taking friends, girls or boys, back to the house knowing that my father would be there gave me a heavy heart (as it did my sister). What would he say? What would he do? That was the problem. Nobody could have answered that question in advance, not even EM. The only certainty was that there would be mischief. Whatever you were doing, he would suddenly appear. One hot afternoon Bill and I discovered a badminton net and racquets inside the garage, and we traipsed around to the back garden to mark out a court of sorts. EM suddenly appeared round a hedge, rather as he made unexpected appearances around the tabs on any number of Morecambe and Wise shows. 'Now what are you doing?' First you'd jump, then you'd laugh, because the way he delivered these little lines commanded laughter.

Anyone who turned up at the house would get the comedy treatment. If I've moaned about anything in my life – and I don't moan much, because I've had a very fortunate life – it's over the matter of my father's interference in the times of my youth. It was fine when we were alone in the house; then he was nothing more or less than my father, we only talked when we needed to, the conversation was reasonably mundane. But as soon as my friends were there he deliberately moved into performance mode. He kept appearing in the room, usually with a question. 'Anyone want a drink?' Off he'd go to the bar. 'Anyone want to watch a Morecambe and Wise video?' He was disruptive in the same way that he was in his act with Ernie. But at home I was Ernie, my friends were the bemused guest stars. EM was totally harmless, and he would have been appalled to think that he was spoiling any fun; he liked young people, and he liked to join in. A line-up of eighteen-year-olds with whiskies and cigars falling around to a Morecambe and Wise video was his idea of heaven. Now I wouldn't have it any other way. Then it drove me crazy.

Of course, my friends didn't see it in the same light. As far as they were concerned, they were getting an Eric Morecambe performance for free – and looking back, I can see how lucky we all were. On my twenty-first birthday in 1977 I tried to keep all my friends separate from the main house by concentrating the party around the swimming pool, where we could have a raucous time. Every so often I'd nip up to the house for civilized conversation with the grown-ups; I thought it was a very practical arrangement. But all any of my friends wanted to talk about was Eric Morecambe, and I ended up spending the whole evening showing him off.

Sometimes having a famous father made it hard to form friendships in the way that I wanted to. On one occasion the front doorbell rang, and EM answered with me a couple of steps behind him. On the doorstep were five young girls: two were my friends, three were their friends. One of them said, 'Hi, Gary!' EM turned to me with a glint in his eye. 'Well, son, it's two and a half each!' This kind of thing was a constant source of irritation in my teens. Living with EM was not automatically as pleasurable as one might assume.

My girlfriends were of natural interest to EM, just as my model aircraft had been a few years earlier.

'So, who's this new girl you're going out with?'

'How do you know about that?'

'Your mother mentioned it.'

'Oh. Just a girl...'

Now EM hated that sort of evasive reply. What he wanted was detail, and the quirkier, the better. Once he asked his usual question, and I replied:

'She's a nurse.'

'Oh, really?' His eyes lit up.

'Yes. And it's very odd, because no matter how much perfume she soaks herself in, she always smells of well-scrubbed hospital floors.'

That was more like it: an image he could get hold of.

'So,' he said, 'when do we meet her?'

It was not unheard of for my girlfriends to come on to EM. I went out one night in my later teens with Bill and a girlfriend I'd known for all of five minutes; we took EM along, because Mum was in Portugal and he was left to fend for himself. As the evening progressed my girlfriend lost control and began rubbing EM's foot with her own stockinged foot. EM said nothing at the time, but afterwards he commented, 'Be careful what you're getting yourself into there, son.' My mother confirms that this sort of thing happened a lot: there were always singers, dancers and so on looking for a chance to get Eric Morecambe. Comedians have great sex appeal because they can make you laugh and feel good; Diana Rigg said something of the sort about EM. It's up to the individual to choose whether or not to deflect the attention or take advantage of it. EM had been in show business for so long that he was immune to advances of this type.

It's another example of a great show-business truism: those who got get more. Success breeds success. You couldn't beat EM; when you're a gifted comedian, the gods favour you. There was little point trying to have an argument or score a point off him; he was always right. We used to argue about music during my teens; I'd be sitting in my bedroom listening to David Bowie when EM would wander in. He'd smile, but in a condescending way, which he knew would always get me going. I rose to the bait every time.

'There's nothing wrong with this!' I'd say belligerently.

'No, no. It's fine,' he'd reply, in a way that said it wasn't fine at all. 'What was that last line he just sang about?'

'Er ... well, I don't know. It doesn't have to be about anything in particular. It's ... it's about things related to his life.'

'Doesn't matter,' said EM. 'He probably just made it up as he went along.' This was rich, considering how much it used to annoy EM when people said the same thing about his work.

It was all gentle, tongue-in-cheek niggling, but he could always get a rise out of me – up to a point. EM knew that after a while I'd just start ignoring him.

To please EM I bought a Duke Ellington album, *Far East Suite*, because I knew he liked it. EM walked in when I'd put it on the turntable for the first time. Instead of the delight I anticipated, he looked bemused. It sounded like Sooty and Sweep fighting over the xylophone.

'What is this nonsense?'

'Surely you like this? It's Duke Ellington. It's one of your favourites.'

'Duke Ellington?' He walked over to the record player and burst out laughing.

'What's wrong?'

'It is Duke Ellington,' said EM, 'but you're playing it at the wrong speed. You're playing it at 78rpm! He must have been in a hurry to get home that night!'

Like I said: you could never win with EM.

Music was a constant bone of contention. EM's tastes were conservative, as you'd imagine: Count Basie, Duke Ellington, Glenn Miller, Eddie Cantor, Gene Kelly, Shirley Bassey, Frank Sinatra, Tony Bennett, his beloved Roger Miller and, later in life, country and western. But every so often you'd look through the pile of eight-track cartridges that he kept in the car and see something totally unexpected – a Frank Zappa album springs to mind. Did he like Frank Zappa? I very much doubt it. Did he have it in his car just to shock people? I should think so.

The generation gap was apparent in more than just our taste in music. EM had very old-fashioned ideas about manners and morals, about dress and behaviour – basically he stuck with the values that he'd been taught by George and Sadie, and he could be very inflexible. When we were little, this manifested itself in his insistence on our dressing smartly and behaving nicely in public, but very little loosened up by the time we were in our teens. He was a stickler for good table manners, and if he saw someone (particularly one of his own children) eating sloppily, he'd tut and frown. He liked you to speak properly as well: the letter T at the end of a word always had to be pronounced, and if you forgot to say 'please' when you'd asked for something he'd wait until you'd said it. If you didn't twig, he'd say 'Per... per...per?' until you said 'please'. Sometimes I wanted to say, 'Per...per...per...piss off'.

Bad language, however, would not have been tolerated. EM was really distressed by anything he considered vulgar, and that applied particularly to language or anything of a sexual nature. He never relaxed on this one; like many of his generation, he couldn't shrug off the semi-Victorian values of his childhood, and swearing always pained him deeply. He found it really offensive. There were no grey areas in his outlook; if he didn't like something, he wasn't prepared to make allowances. I remember him watching one of the last films of Burt Lancaster – an actor of EM's own generation, whom he greatly admired – in which there was a lot of swearing. It really upset EM to hear Burt Lancaster swear; he felt let down in some way, betrayed. A fellow old-timer in show business had crossed the line between acceptable and unacceptable. The fact that Lancaster was an actor and was playing a role didn't enter the equation. EM's world was more about people bursting into song and dance, about escapism and fantasy; he found the vogue for realism hard to embrace.

I've inherited some of this, I realize. I find myself tutting over what I consider to be 'gratuitous' bad language in comedy, or on-screen sex. I can't pinpoint exactly what unsettles me, and I imagine that my children think I'm an old fuddy-duddy, but it's obviously to do with my upbringing.

EM was not above telling people off if he thought they were overstepping the mark. Driving through Harpenden, he'd roll down the window if he saw a couple canoodling in the street and shout, 'What are you doing? Go home to do that sort of thing!' It was partly a gag, but he meant it as well.

One Sunday afternoon I caught my thumb in a drawer, and whispered 'Oh, fuck!' to myself – and it was to myself, because as far as I was aware I was alone in my own room. I hadn't heard my mother by the airing cupboard on the landing, and obviously she was shocked by the expletive. Later on EM challenged me about it. 'You mustn't use words like that, you know,' he said. He really worried about this sort of thing; he didn't want me to become part of what he saw as a problem of modern society. His need to castigate me, however moderate, was nonetheless genuine. It was a defining moment in my teenage development and I realized that I'd have to develop a kind of double persona – one that suited his particular ethics and one for my 'real' life outside the home. There was nothing to be gained by trying to blend the two worlds except frustration. I comprehended that fact in a flash at the age of fourteen.

You only had to look at EM to see that he was what my generation would call 'uptight'. There's a photograph of Eric and Ernie on Blackpool beach in 1952: both are in shirt sleeves, but Ernie retains his tie, while Eric is sporting a cravat. In the background are men wearing suits; if it was hot, they might remove the jacket. 'Casual' wear just hadn't been invented when he was a young man. A generation on, young people were wearing T-shirts and jeans, but EM never came to terms with this. He bumped into Roy Hudd some time in the early eighties, when they were both on their way to a radio studio, and both were smartly dressed in jackets and ties. 'Do you realize,' said EM, 'that we're probably the only ones left who still dress for radio?'

Even around the house he usually wore a jacket and tie. This persisted right through the seventies, but relaxed a little in the eighties, when he started to wear baggy jumpers and even, on occasion, tracksuit bottoms.

A crucial link with EM's past was broken in 1976 when his father, George, died suddenly. His mind had been playing tricks on him for a while, which made life difficult for Sadie and the rest of the family; on one occasion he accused my father of stealing some non-existent trout out of the freezer and hiding them. Then, one evening in his sitting room, he stood up, shouted 'Sadie!' and was dead by the time he hit the ground.

After the funeral we brought Sadie back to live with us in Harpenden. In the car on the way home she was absolutely inconsolable. 'I'm leaving him behind!' she cried. 'It's wrong!'

'No, you're not, Mum,' said EM, who was very philosophical about George's death. 'You mustn't see it like that. You can come back any time you like to visit him.'

Sadie declined rapidly over the next year; she didn't want to be with us, she wanted to be back in the north, back with George. Dead together was definitely preferable to living apart. As EM remarked, 'She's convinced she'll sit on a fluffy cloud with Dad, with angels in the background playing harps.' She died the following year. For the last few months my mother was her nurse. Gail was with Sadie when she died; I was out at work, and to be honest I was glad to miss that scene. It was just before my twenty-first birthday, and a couple of days earlier she had said to me, 'Last night I dreamed I died. And you know what? The only thing I was worried about was that I hadn't signed your birthday cheque in time.'

On the evening of Sadie's death I returned from work to find EM calmly watching TV, smoking his pipe. Nothing seemed to have changed. I gave him a big hug – a rare thing – and told him how sorry I was to hear about Sadie. He just nodded and said 'Yes, well, she had a good innings.' And that, it seemed, was that.

About 10.30 p.m. he told my mother and me that he was off to bed. He slunk out of the room and we passed a few comments about what a strain it must be for him as Sadie had been his mother, his mentor and the creator of Morecambe and Wise. Two minutes later he silently returned and hugged my mother a bit and then burst into tears.

We drove Sadie's body back to Lancashire in the back of the family Volvo estate – a car she'd loved driving around in to nowhere in particular.

'Who knows,' said EM, 'if we keep the car for long enough, it might be my body in the back of it next time.'

Seven years later EM's driver, Mike, and I transported my father's body from Cheltenham Hospital to the undertakers in Harpenden in the back of the very same Volvo estate.

chapter 10

In 1973 I was sixteen with little to show for the time I had spent at boarding school other than a small handful of 'O' levels. I spent most of my time moping around the family home and feeling very much as if the halcyon days of my youth were now over. The family holidays would continue for a while longer, but they would feel less like holidays and more like opportunities to delay confronting the future.

It had only been a couple of years since I'd gone with my parents and Gail on a cruise aboard the recently launched *QE2*. Ernie and his wife Doreen were on the cruise too, implying there was a work-related reason for us travelling together. Interestingly, this was the only time Eric and Ernie went on the same holiday at the same time. They didn't actively avoid each other over the following ten days, but they were conscious of moving around each other and being seen regularly in each other's company. I don't know what Ernie made of it, but EM was often accosted with questions like 'Are you looking for Ernie?' Good-humouredly he'd reply, 'No, I've got him in my pocket!' But looking back, it must have felt pretty banal and tiring.

Two years on, and taking holidays wasn't a priority in my life. I tried doing an 'O' level in art, as that was one subject I hadn't taken at school, and I failed that too – very depressing. I couldn't even blame a lack of interest in academia; I put everything I had into that exam and it wasn't enough. To make matters worse, EM was very good at painting, as is my sister.

I had to do something, and my mother and I decided that St Alban's College of Further Education would be a useful place to be for the next couple of years. It wasn't the most exciting of establishments. I'd escaped school, true, but college was only marginally freer. It was still academia, it was still about attending lessons, except now they were called lectures. (I thought that was very cool – for about three days.) It was co-ed, which was a pleasant change from the all-boys environment of Aldenham, but even that novelty wore thin after a week or two. All the girls seemed to have mysterious boyfriends in the outside world, and they weren't interested in their fellow students. I studied for an OND in business studies – and at the end of two years I failed that as well.

The best thing about college was that, for the first time in my life, I was in an ordinary environment, among people from ordinary backgrounds. I was teased a little about my private education, but not much; that was soon pretty valueless when our law lecturer gave away a far greater secret in his first address to the class.

'Which of you is Eric Morecambe's son?'

He spotted me, as I reluctantly raised a hand.

'Ah. I'm a great fan of your father.'

I never knew how he found out my 'secret', as I'd naively hoped to keep EM to myself for the duration of the course. Inevitably I succeeded only for two days.

One of the other students turned round and said, 'Christ!

We've got royalty here! Why's someone like you coming to an ordinary dump like this?'

I couldn't think of an answer at the time, and just shrugged. Ask me the question now, though, and I'd say that it was because I was no different from them; I was the son of a famous comedian, but I wasn't a famous comedian myself. Like most of them, I didn't know where the future would take me. This 'dump' was as good a starting place as any. I was treading water while the spotty face sorted itself out. I was hopeless at the work, more interested in listening to David Bowie and Lou Reed and going on pub crawls. The weeks floated past. I divided my time between drinking and attending enough lectures to prevent myself from being thrown off the course.

And I learned to type. The only boy in a class of fifteen. Embarrassed? Yes, but with hindsight deeply grateful to whatever inspired me to go ahead and lose a lot of street cred with my male peers. And I was used to being the only boy. My primary school days had seen to that!

EM paid a visit to the college during my last months there. I don't know where the idea came from – certainly not from me. But he went along with it, which was generous of him, and of course it went down very well. The basic format was question and answer, like 'An Audience with Eric Morecambe'. EM loved the idea. It was an opportunity to go over his life story, dropping in the funnies when appropriate, working completely off-script. It's a format he returned to later in life; in fact, he was doing a show exactly like that the night he died.

Fortunately for me, I had a job lined up for when I left college, which is just as well because I came out of St Alban's with nothing to show for the two years I'd been there apart from a lot of practice driving between pubs. It had been suggested a couple of years earlier that I might get a job with EM's agent Billy Marsh, and increasingly that was what I focused my energies on. It was this that prompted me to take that typing course during the last months of my OND course.

Billy Marsh was looking for an able young man to replace his recently departed protégé, a certain Michael Grade, who still regards Billy as his greatest mentor. At the time Billy was planning to set up an internal publicity unit to work with his clients, among whom were Morecambe and Wise; that unit turned out to be me and my colleague Eddie Waters, who worked part-time for Billy, part-time as a photo-journalist and picture editor for the *Sun*. Eddie had show-business connections himself – he's the nephew of the wartime radio double act, Elsie and Doris Waters, and also of Jack Warner of *Dixon of Dock Green* fame – so we had a lot in common. (And, just in case he wasn't busy enough, Eddie went on to become EM's literary agent.)

So now I was part of the commuting masses, travelling in every day from Harpenden to Billy's office at the Oxford Circus end of Regent Street. On my first day I was taken out for lunch in a pub somewhere near Liberty's – and this lunch finished around 4pm, about the time the double vision started. Eddie, who was remarkably sober, suggested we should go back to the office and type up some notes. I could hardly see the typewriter, let alone the notes. Eddie took one look at the rubbish I'd typed up and agreed it might be better to start again in the morning.

I staggered back on to the train, fell asleep, missed my stop and woke up in Luton. When I finally got home, EM took one look at me and said, 'How could you go and drink too much on your first day at work?' He ranted a bit and began laying down the law, which was fair enough seeing as I was working for his agent in a job that, basically, EM had secured for me. And then, with perfect timing and absolutely no sense of irony, he deadpanned, 'Now – how about a drink? What do you fancy?' When I told Billy the next day he fell about laughing. He'd repeat the story at every opportunity, concluding with EM's punchline. It became his party piece.

I loved working for Billy Marsh. He was a show-business giant – he knew everyone who mattered in that period, and I was very lucky to know him. He'd started off working for Bernard Delfont, Lew Grade's brother, before setting up in Oxford Street with Leslie Grade, Lew's other brother and Michael Grade's father.

Eric and Ernie would often pop in for a meeting with Billy, and they'd always stick their heads round my door. EM would always make a joke about my clothes, because he didn't think I dressed appropriately for office life. I would drift in and out of Billy's office to carry messages or, more often, to join them for a whisky. I was uncomfortable with this preferential treatment, which never goes down well in an office environment, but no one ever gave me a hard time. In fact, our working lives were one long laugh; the office became known as the Fun Factory. Sometimes after a few whiskies Billy would ask me to go next door to Verry's restaurant for a bite to eat, oblivious to the fact that I was anxious to get home to Harpenden in time for dinner. I didn't like to let him down, so I never refused.

One afternoon I was sitting in Billy's office with EM, and between the three of us we'd polished off the best part of a bottle of whisky. EM and Billy started fantasizing about the worst possible publicity that could come their way.

'I've got it,' said EM, snapping his fingers. 'Gary has an affair with a well-known woman twice his age.'

'A well-known divorced woman,' said Billy.

'A well-known divorced woman with three kids,' said EM.

'Three kids about the same age as Gary,' said Billy.

EM looked at me and laughed. 'There's no need to look quite so keen on the idea, you know.'

Billy represented a lot of big TV names in the seventies. I once shared the lift with Bruce Forsyth, who didn't have a clue who I was but saw the briefcase in my hand.

'Are you selling brushes?' he asked.

Working for a theatrical agency where your father is the biggest piece of business is a strange experience. Even stranger were the times when I worked directly for him in my role as a publicity officer.

My main purpose in being at the Floral Hall was to sell posters and T-shirts of Morecambe and Wise. During all my time at Billy Marsh's office, this had to be the strangest of feelings. It was one thing to find myself working in a Morecambe and Wise environment, but to be selling merchandise of my own father!

Everyone was always kind to me at the theatres, and on this occasion I was placed in the foyer just as the doors opened prior to the evening performance. The shirts, more than the posters, used to sell in bucket loads, and as I passed them over to customer after customer, it more than once crossed my mind how surprised they would be to learn that this spotty teenage salesman with long hair was, in fact, the son of half the act they had paid up to see that night.

After the allocated sale time was up, I would always be approached by people in the business who did know exactly who I was. It was a little akin to being back at school again where I learned almost immediately to sense what my peers were after. Now, as an adult in the employ of Mr Marsh, I discovered that what various people wanted from me – and they were agents every one of them – was to bend my ear about their act so I could apply pressure on EM to get them a shot on a Morecambe and Wise show. No better way to reach millions, so I could understand the logic.

'Come and have a drink, Gary,' would be the usual opener. And I would go along with it, because we were acting out a game – to the extent that I now think that they knew that I knew what they were up to!

But I'd never be forced into a corner. 'Yes, he's a great magician!' 'Yes, she's a great singer!' 'Yes, they're a great duo!' And by making positive comments like that, whatever I might truly have thought of the act in question, they were less inclined to push much further, believing that enough pressure had been applied.

Occasionally it happened that an act did blow me away, and I couldn't wait to tell EM. The blues singer, Madeline Bell, springs to mind. She was represented by Billy Marsh's office and I saw her perform at what was then The Talk of

The Town - now Stringfellows. EM listened to my praise and put her on a Morecambe and Wise bill for a Royal Show for HRH Prince Charles – who, it transpired, was a big fan.

During my years at Billy Marsh's, I became distracted by a mad idea: I wanted to be a rock star. The fact that I couldn't sing or play an instrument didn't seem to matter, nor did the fact that I had one of the most famous fathers in the country – and it's very rare for the children of a famous parent to make it in anything like the same arena. I just thought it would be a lot cooler than working in a theatrical office.

I decided to take six months off – and EM was staggered by my decision. The idea of walking out of a good job was absolutely insane to him, and in retrospect I can see his point, but it took me six months of aimless meandering with semi-musical figures to discover what he already knew. Fortunately for me, Billy was very understanding, and would never stand in the way of anyone's self-expression, and so he gave me six months' unpaid leave with the promise of a job at the end of it.

As quickly as I said goodbye, I said hello again. There was a general air of 'We wondered when you'd be back' about it all, which was very embarrassing, but I took it in good spirit. You have to learn by your mistakes, after all. EM was tolerant, but he remained constantly bemused. During my sabbatical I composed a dreadful song called 'When the Wind Blows'. 'You've got to be careful with a title like that,' said EM. 'Sounds like someone with a stomach complaint.'

It wasn't entirely a waste of time. I discovered how much I enjoyed working for Billy. I discovered, as the inhibited son of an extrovert parent, that I did have a creative voice, if not a singing one. It was a step on the road to finding out what I wanted to do – although it probably also had something to do with being lazy and bored and fancying six months off.

Of more significance in the long run was the fact that my job at Billy's gave me the first opportunity to do a bit of writing. In my role as publicist I had to revise and update the touring programme that Morecambe and Wise sold at the various theatres; I chose the photos and wrote the biographies. I saw the final print in the office and I loved it – but on the way home I started to get worried. Would EM like it? Some of the quotes attributed to him had been written by me; would he approve? To my relief, he looked it over and said, 'Great. You've done a really good job. I'm glad they've given you a credit.' Then he went back to watching TV. I was chuffed to bits, but just responded with, 'Good. I'm pleased you like it,' as if it was just one of many bits of creative work I'd run off that day.

I spent a good deal of 1978 out of the office, touring around the country with the various acts that Billy Marsh represented. One of these was that wily old fox Basil Brush – who was, in reality, a man called Ivan Owen, crouched awkwardly beneath a desk with a TV monitor. Basil Brush did a winter season at the Victoria Palace, London, and I spent much of the time with Ivan.

Ivan wasn't averse to a drink or two, and we could often be found in the pub together. One day I said, 'You know, Ivan, I'm a really big fan of yours.'

He shook his head. 'Oh go on, you're just saying that.'

'No, I'm not...'

'Well, someone just did. Boom! Boom!' Then that huge Basil Brush laugh, me blushing and the pub falling silent as they listened to the familiar sounds of this unfamiliar man.

The late seventies saw the final death of the variety circuit in Great Britain, and working for Billy Marsh I was lucky enough to witness the tail end of a formerly great tradition. It's not easy trying to explain to my children why it had once been such a popular form of entertainment – even harder to explain why we persevered with it after it was clearly dead. But variety was the first form of mass entertainment, long before TV and video, before cinema, before radio even. And it was special to me, because it was the birthplace of Morecambe and Wise. It had simply outstayed its welcome.

It was a tough time for comedians trying to make the transition from the variety circuit to television. EM was always grateful that he'd had 'somewhere to go where you can be bad', as he put it. The comedy club circuit of today didn't yet exist, so there weren't the venues that nurtured the likes of Ben Elton, Rik Mayall, Harry Hill, Alexei Sayle and Jo Brand. Even now, with a flourishing comedy circuit, television consumes those talents very quickly. For Morecambe and Wise to get from their first footsteps on a variety stage to their first TV series took twenty years: that's twenty years before they got down to the career for which they would be remembered. That's one of the reasons they were so good – they'd had time to nurture their act, to learn from their mistakes without exposing them to huge TV audiences. By the time they were on screen they'd had so much practice that they could turn even mistakes to their advantage. Young comedians who don't have that experience are terribly vulnerable, and TV audiences are not forgiving.

In 1978 I was at the Poole Arts Centre in Dorset for a

summer season with Leslie Crowther. It was a wretched show even by the standards of the late seventies – weak comedy routines and speciality acts were interspersed with limply choreographed dance numbers. It stank of a different era: of tea rooms and cloth caps and whelks on the beach. From my experience of variety as a child I could recognize a form of entertainment from a bygone era that had lost all its sharpness and vitality. Variety was dying, and promoters were looking for a fresh alternative.

It was towards television that everyone was looking. Leslie Crowther himself concentrated on hosting *The Price is Right*, while Billy Marsh's future summer seasons drew almost exclusively on TV talent – Keith Harris and Orville, Basil Brush, Rolf Harris, the Three Degrees. The old school of entertainers, who came up through the music halls and learned their craft in front of live theatre audiences, was a thing of the past.

Billy put on a show in Bradford attended by Princess Anne. One of my jobs was to meet Arthur Askey off the train and carry his bags to the hotel. To me Arthur represented the past – I didn't find him at all funny, but it was nonetheless a privilege to walk down the street with a man who, for his generation, was an icon of entertainment. Once he found out that my father was Eric Morecambe, the conversation flowed. Arthur had worked with Ernie Wise sixteen years before I was born, of course, and he knew of the great regard in which EM held him. Arthur viewed Morecambe and Wise as a headmaster might view a favourite student who had gone on to great things.

On the night of the show I was introduced to Princess

Anne, who was also keen to talk about Morecambe and Wise. When she met Ivan Owen, who was holding Basil Brush in one arm, he asked her, 'Have you fallen off any good horses recently?'

'You don't fall off the good ones,' she replied, quick as a flash.

A year later, at another show, I was introduced to Prince Charles. 'Tell me,' he said, 'is your side of the business more lucrative than your father's?'

'I wish it was, sir,' was all I could think of to reply.

In 1979 I met Tracey; a year later she would become my wife. It was time to move on, and I left Billy Marsh. We kept in touch for the rest of his life, for he was always more of a friend than an employer, and I was always more the son of a favourite comic than an employee. I would go so far as to say that I was as close to Billy as were either Eric or Ernie.

For a time in 1982 Billy and I considered working on his autobiography, but he came to the conclusion that there were just too many of his former clients still alive for him to tell any of his best stories.

Billy was very supportive to me at EM's funeral in 1984. He was light and friendly, knowing what I was going through. He didn't think about the fact that he'd lost a client of twenty years; he just did anything he could to lessen the family's grief.

When Billy died in 1996, it didn't hit me at first. Then, about a week later, I was driving home when some memory of a distant moment or conversation came back to me, and I had to pull over while I got myself together.

Billy's clients passed on to his successor, Jan Kennedy –

and, in terms of Morecambe and Wise, it was absolutely seamless. Jan looked after Billy in his declining years, and soaked up his knowledge. I often think of her as Billy Marsh incarnate.

chapter II

Morecambe and Wise moved from the BBC to Thames Television in 1978. The decision was not, as a lot of people have suggested over the years, money-motivated; they went to Thames because they'd been offered the chance by the company's movie wing, Euston Films, to make something for the big screen. They'd wanted to do this for some time, if only to eclipse their three outings for Rank Films in the sixties.

EM warmly embraced the change of channels. He felt they'd done their best work for the BBC, and that it was time to move on to pastures new. Also he'd been unsettled by a fan letter, which congratulated Eric and Ernie on a decade of wonderful shows but suggested that it was time they called it a day as their material and performances were palling. 'What do you reckon?' he asked, waving the letter under my nose.

'Well,' I said, 'there's bound to be a similarity in the shows as they work to a specific format.'

'That means you agree with the writer of the letter, then?'

'No, but I understand his point.'

EM shrugged. 'If this sort of reaction becomes common, then I'll know it's time to quit.' And that was all that was ever said on the matter. It was always a touchy subject. As early as 1973 Eric and Ernie had said they were concerned with the repetitive format of their shows; this was one of the reasons they brought in Ernest Maxin as a producer, so that they could use his choreographic skills to introduce more musical numbers into the shows. The switch back to ITV was, therefore, in part an attempt to freshen up the act, to meet some new challenges and create some new work. People generally feel now that the shows they did for Thames weren't as good as those they did for the BBC; certainly Morecambe and Wise were getting older by this time, and they no longer had Eddie Braben with them to write the scripts.

It may seem strange that a performer as successful as EM was in 1978 should be affected by the comments of a fan, but he always took that sort of thing to heart: he had a constant need for reassurance, and he was sensitive to criticism. This stemmed from a basic insecurity about his work; he knew that people liked what he did, but there was always a lurking doubt that somehow his profession was not 'for real'. Ernie, I think, viewed his profession as an honourable one, but for EM there was an element of 'well, it beats doing a real job...' He never rid himself of that feeling that he was 'just a clown'. Jan Kennedy reminded me of a time when she was sitting in Billy Marsh's office with Eric and Ernie, when EM suddenly said, 'But what if they find us out?' He meant it too: he had this fear that the public would one day see through him, and that his success would be taken away. Such success, he felt, comes at a price. It was the winning-the-lottery angle to their career. This doubt gnawed at him from the moment Morecambe and Wise started their TV career; success came quickly, and it could disappear just as fast. Those of us who are old enough to remember Simon Dee and his *Dee Time*

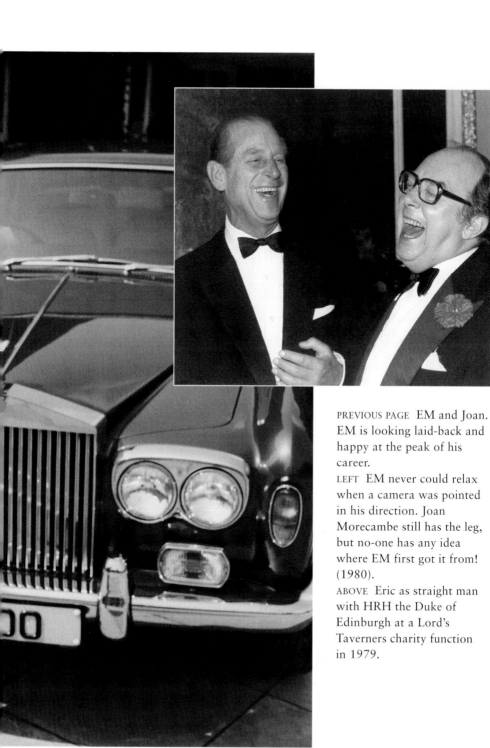

PREVIOUS PAGE EM and Joan.
EM is looking laid-back and
happy at the peak of his
career.

LEFT EM never could relax
when a camera was pointed
in his direction. Joan
Morecambe still has the leg,
but no-one has any idea
where EM first got it from!
(1980).

ABOVE Eric as straight man
with HRH the Duke of
Edinburgh at a Lord's
Taverners charity function
in 1979.

ABOVE EM with Gary in 1982, discussing their first ever joint venture – a book promotional tour.

RIGHT Christmas 1983 with Steven. EM always had to hand out presents at Christmas, and sadly this was to be the last time he did it before he died.

TOP LEFT EM with grandchildren Amelia and Adam on Amelia's fourth birthday. Unfortunately, EM didn't live long enough to meet his other four grandchildren.
TOP RIGHT EM in his garden.
ABOVE EM, EW and Benny Hill with Hill's Angels Sue Upton and Trudi Miller at a Thames TV bash to celebrate the duo's arrival at Thames (Lincolns Inn, *c*1978).

ABOVE The *Night Train to Murder* cast 1983, with Lysette Anthony (2nd from left) and Fulton Mackay (3rd from right). The film was meant to eclipse their Rank outings, but didn't even make it to the big screen.

RIGHT EM, Joan and Gary on holiday in Florida in 1983 after EM had transferred his allegiance from Portugal to America.

BELOW Hamish McColl, Gary, Sean Foley (doing an Eric) and Toby Jones – the men behind *The Play What I Wrote*, Wyndham's Theatre, 2002.
BOTTOM LEFT Joan with Magdi Yacoub, who performed the heart surgery on EM.
BOTTOM RIGHT Gary with Gail, summer 2002, at the old family home.
OVERLEAF Seven feet tall in bronze, EM returns to Morecambe Bay.

show will know that there was some basis to this fear.

This was a time of great change in our family – not just because Morecambe and Wise had moved from the BBC to ITV, but also because I finally moved out of the family home at the age of twenty-two. I'd left Billy Marsh's office, and together with Tracey, my future wife, I moved up to Huntingdon, Cambridgeshire, to help run the family business. That business was two small hotels, the Golden Lion in St Ives and the Tudor in Fenstanton, about three miles apart, which belonged to my mother and her publican brother, Alan Bartlett. EM had a vested interest in the business, but it was primarily my mother's concern (and at the time of writing she still owns the Golden Lion). I went to work behind the bar, which gave me plenty of time to think about what I wanted to do with my life. Tracey and I lived in rented accommodation, and spent weekends either visiting her parents in Somerset, or going home to Harpenden. Eventually we bought our first house together, Three Horseshoes Cottage, which was strategically placed in a hamlet quite near the hotels. It was a former pub with a thatched roof and a pretty garden surrounded by fields.

EM came to visit the hotels occasionally for lunch. It was always good to see him, but I never felt fully comfortable with him drifting around the place. He was good with the customers, saying the funny lines they wanted to hear and so on, but it was uneasy for me having him in my place of work. It hadn't mattered during the Billy Marsh years, as we were both then involved in show business, but here in the hotel it was different. I was trying to learn a new trade, and he was unfamiliar with it. Also, as he had financed the hotels in the first place, there was a sense that he was the big boss breathing down my neck.

I quickly came to realize that I was not cut out for the hotel trade. I got orders wrong, and it's amazing any of the staff was paid. Residents would arrive to find beds unmade – mind you, that wasn't entirely my fault, as we discovered our elderly cleaning lady out cold in the toilet with several empty bottles of barley wine by her side. The first hotel we worked at, the Golden Lion, while not exactly a den of iniquity, was a regular pick-up joint for straights and gays alike. Then there was the couple who checked into the hotel one afternoon, stole the television and left without paying. Another couple checked in, had sex in the room and left. A commercial traveller demanded to be moved because he'd seen a ghost in his room and was turning into a nervous wreck. By this time so was I. I had reached the unforgivable conclusion that all the customers were complete idiots, so it was probably time for me to find a different job. And to top it all, Tracey had a slight misfortune on Christmas Day when she was waitressing and poured an entire turkey dinner over one unlucky gentleman. He took it very well, considering. That incident seemed to sum up the way our hotel career was going – and before long new managers were employed.

Just before my short involvement with the family hotel business, EM had his second heart attack. The warning signs were all there: all through 1977 and 1978 his behaviour had been erratic. He'd get moody with his driver, Mike Fountain, or with me, if we left him too long signing autographs at a charity function. Usually he took pleasure in conversing with the public, but I remember one occasion when he came out of a Lord's Taverners' do with a face like thunder.

'What the hell are you playing at? I thought my own flaming son would know better.'

'What's the matter?'

'Why the hell didn't you come in and get me? I've been trying to get away for about an hour, while you've been sitting here doing nothing.'

'It's our fault. I'm sorry,' said Mike, knowing the only thing to do was to calm EM down. Why had he flown off the handle? What had riled him about being in a place he liked, with people he liked, doing charity work that he'd chosen to do? Mike told me later that EM had flashes of this temperament all through 1978 and into 1979; when put in the context of his general health, which was deteriorating, it makes sense.

And EM was never the most relaxed of people. My mother described him as a bundle of nervous energy. 'Sometimes unable to sit down long enough to finish a meal.'

A theatrical agent told me that once he took EM out for dinner with Benny Hill in a not-very-salubrious part of London. EM was so uncomfortable, he hardly ate anything and spoke very little.

One afternoon in the summer of 1978 I was playing a record in his study when the phone rang. I was slow to turn the volume down, and after he'd finished the call he started swearing at me. Now this was a sure sign that something was wrong; EM, as I've mentioned, hated swearing and never did it.

One morning in January 1979 EM and I were standing in the kitchen at home. He opened the fridge, I heard a clattering sound, turned round and there he was, prostrate on the tiled floor in his dressing gown, pale and hardly conscious. He came round quickly.

'What happened?'

'You fell. This floor's slippery.'

'No. I blacked out for a moment.'

I heard warning bells. 'Do you want me to call a doctor?'

EM was sweating buckets. 'My heart's beating so fast. Yes, call a doctor.'

Soon EM was on his way to hospital, where it became clear that he'd had another serious heart attack – and this time he needed surgery. Without the triple bypass, he had only months, perhaps weeks, to live.

I went to visit him in Harefield Hospital just before his surgery. He viewed the situation with great fortitude, which put me at my ease. We took a gentle stroll round the grounds, talking about comedy and books, then EM said, 'I got very upset last night. Silly, really. I started to feel sorry for myself, and I began to cry. I kept wondering, why me?'

'That's quite natural,' I told him.

'Yes, but then I realized that I've had so much. You can't have everything in this life. Then I was all right.'

I dreaded having to say goodbye, but at the same time I couldn't wait to get away from the place. I have never enjoyed going to hospitals for any reason, including even the birth of my own children. I recall the image of EM standing in the doorway of the hospital waving at me, like the proud owner of a new mansion house.

On the night of my father's operation I was at a party in Somerset. I felt terrible. What was I doing there, when I should have been at EM's side? I behaved oddly, and it was particularly tough on Tracey, who was trying to catch up with some old friends from her past. But everything went well, thanks to Professor Magdi Yacoub and his team at Harefield Hospital, who gave EM another five years of life.

It all seemed to be over so quickly: EM slumped on the kitchen floor, EM waving me off from the hospital, then EM back home recovering from his surgery and returning to work.

EM used his convalescence to do something he'd been meaning to try for some time: he wrote a novel. He'd been thinking about it for some years; in fact, he'd written one a few years before, when I was working at Billy Marsh's office – a comedy cowboy story set in nineteenth-century America. At the time EM had written nothing outside Morecambe and Wise scripts, and it seemed an odd starting point for a budding novelist, and I told him so. Furthermore, it was plain bizarre. I recall one line which ran: 'He walked along the main street sensing something was dead. Then he realized what it was. It was the town.' In retrospect, this doesn't seem as bad as it did at the time.

A family friend, the publisher Christopher Falkus, was talking to us at a London book launch one evening.

'You really should try your hand at a novel, Eric.'

'Yes,' said EM, glancing my way, 'I've thought about it. I had an idea for a comedy cowboy story, but Gary read some of it and thought it was terrible.'

'Let's be honest, Dad,' I said, 'it was awful.'

'I suppose it was,' said EM. 'In any case, I never finished it...'

'But the story doesn't matter,' said Chris. 'It's the comedy, and the fact that it's by Eric Morecambe, that will make it work.'

EM's ears pricked up. 'Really?'

'Without question.'

They both looked at me, and I wanted the ground to swallow me up. Later that evening, EM said to me:

'You see? I could have had a book published. You put me off the idea.'

By the time EM was recovering from his heart attack and having another go at writing, he'd found a much more suitable subject for a comic writing a novel: *Mr Lonely* was about a stand-up comedian. It took some months to write, as EM had been advised to get plenty of rest and not over-stimulate his mind following the surgery, so he wrote only when he was feeling up to it, a couple of hours a day at most. When I was visiting Harpenden, which was quite often during this period, he'd emerge from his study with a dozen pages and read them to me. 'What do you think?' he'd ask. I'd learnt my lesson by now.

'I think it's brilliant, Dad. It's the best extract from a novel of its kind I've ever read.'

His eyes lit up. 'Did you hear that, Joan? Tell Mum what you said.'

'Yes,' said my mother diplomatically, 'it's certainly coming along...'

I'm still uncertain about *Mr Lonely*. It was a brave undertaking, and the fact that it's full of Eric Morecambe-isms is a big plus. I tried, once, to make a gentle criticism of the book, based on the fact that it seemed to be too full of his TV persona, but EM understood that the public would never accept him as an author, that however many books he wrote he would always be, primarily, the TV comedian Eric Morecambe writing a book. Now, when just about any comedian can write a novel, we know that what sells isn't the content of the pages but the name on the cover. EM understood that the product had to fit in with the persona; he was perceptive in that respect.

I think this extract shows just how much of EM there was in the book:

He was now looking into the face of Mr Nolan's secretary, a woman with a figure like a cornflake box, economy size. Her name was Bonnie, which she wasn't. Her hair looked like two pounds of straight candles. Her eyes observed Sid the same way a just-wakened boa constrictor looks at a fat, juicy rabbit. He felt he was standing in the way of Charles Bronson in lipstick. She was the epitome of that wonderful saying, 'She was the good time had by nobody'. She pushed Sid to one side as she looked up and down the corridor for the tea lady. 'Where's the tea lady?' she bawled. 'Who shouted "TEA"?'

'Hello, I'm looking for Mr Nolan,' said Sid.

'Who shouted "Tea", eh? Who was it? Answer me! Who shouted tea?' She came out of the office into the corridor. Sid looked into the office and saw Mr Nolan. Ivor waved a 'come in'. He was still on the phone. Sid walked in and was immediately attacked from behind by Bonnie. She grabbed his arm in a vice-like grip and bellowed, 'What are you doing in this room?'

'I have an appointment with Mr Nolan.' Sid tried to blink away the tears as he slowly went towards the ground. He looked at her hand gripping his arm muscle. Her knuckles were whiter than a learner driver's. He tried to shake her off, but she hung on like the British bulldog she resembled...

To EM, books represented his working future. He always thought that if he, or Ernie, or the public, had ever had enough of Morecambe and Wise, he could turn to writing books as a second career. Instead it became a useful way of filling in the time during the various blips in his health. He had found a new field in which to express himself, a field in which he could learn new things and experiment with new ideas. It was far removed from the rigours of performing in a comedy double act. It kept him in touch with his public, but without the pressure of actively being Morecambe and Wise.

By the end of 1979 *Mr Lonely* was taking shape and EM was getting back into shape. We were entering the period of the false dawn, when, once again, we believed that we were witnessing the full and everlasting recovery of Eric Morecambe. Or rather we chose to believe it. A pattern had formed: the illness, the recovery, the great success, the illness again. It was strangely comfortable; it allowed us to believe that he would always get better.

The professional results of the heart attack were obvious: EM wasn't up to performing a Morecambe and Wise Christmas show in 1979, so instead he and Ernie went on a Christmas night chat show with David Frost. It was a real tonic for EM – a trip down memory lane, with clips of their earlier work and a couple of new routines, one with Glenda Jackson performed live for the studio audience.

There were personal repercussions to the heart attack as

well. EM became more serious. Out for a meal, he gagged less with the waiters, he didn't mess around doing funnies during the meal, he didn't do his favourite trick of stealing someone's wine when they were out of the room, drinking it and then claiming he knew nothing about it. I don't know if this was a change for the better – it was just a change, that's all. He was more interested in conversation; he always liked to talk, but now he liked to listen as well. He was less likely to interrupt with a comic line. These were mellow days. Instead of pretending to collapse with a knife in his chest, or pretending his thumb was caught in the menu when he handed it back to the waiter, or thrusting a bread roll under your nose and saying, 'Will you say a few words, please?' he'd just relax and enjoy himself.

He was still happy to talk about comedy, but there was nothing left for him to prove, and it no longer formed an obsession for him. He was dedicated to entertaining people, but no longer to the exclusion of all else. His health mattered more, and he didn't have the energy to go at it full throttle any more. He was under doctors' orders to rethink his life, and in a way he did – although not to the extent that the doctors would have liked. On reflection, he should never have returned to comedy after his bypass surgery. If someone had said to him, 'That's really it, Eric. No more comedy. It will kill you if you continue,' he would have stopped before the sentence was finished. But nobody ever said that. There was a mistaken belief that EM couldn't live without being a professional funny guy. Ten years earlier that might have been true; not now, though. Not after surgery.

By the end of 1980 EM was fully recovered. When Tracey

and I were married he came to our wedding, and he was on top form. He'd given up alcohol and tobacco, and it showed in the way he looked, the sharpness of his mind. It was truly uplifting to see him so well less than two years after heart surgery.

More surprising was the fact that a year after being so close to death, he was back at Thames Television making shows with Ernie Wise. For years I thought the material they did for Thames was much weaker than the BBC stuff, but then, a couple of years ago, I was involved in putting together a series of highlights from those shows, re-edited and with new graphics. I was astounded; it was right up there with their BBC shows. Admittedly you had to wade through a lot more material to get to the gems, whereas the consistency of the BBC shows was remarkable – but gems there were. The six half-hour highlights shows we put together for Thames were wonderful entertainment, as good as anything Morecambe and Wise ever did.

I tried to keep up to date with Morecambe and Wise, and to visit the Thames studios in Teddington to watch them record a show, but I didn't get there as often as I'd have liked; I was split between Cambridge and Tracey's family in Somerset, so time was short. What struck me at Teddington was the atmosphere – far more relaxed than it had ever been at the BBC. I wouldn't go so far as to suggest that Eric and Ernie regarded this as the twilight of their career, but there was definitely a sense that they could almost have worked in their sleep, so well did they know what they were doing. EM would contest this, and always claimed that he needed to be revved up to do his best work – but if you look at some of the footage that didn't make the highlights series, you'll see that for a lot of the time EM was distinctly not revved up. He had to be more subdued following his heart attack – and the surgery had definitely had an effect on his general demeanour. Their producer of old, Johnny Ammonds, told me that he thought EM's comic timing was going, and believed this was a direct result of the surgery. He further confessed to having to edit their material, particularly EM's, to make it work at all – something unheard of in the past. I think that if Morecambe and Wise had continued working together, the standard would have dropped to a catastrophic low.

Much of this was due to a paucity of new material; without Eddie Braben writing their scripts, Eric and Ernie were forced to take material they'd performed ten years earlier for the BBC and regurgitate it for Thames. The defining moment was when Hannah Gordon appeared on the Thames show in a sketch that was almost identical to her appearance years ago on the BBC – EM even repeated his line 'Hello, Miss Gordon. I drink all your gin.' The problem with repetition is that it just draws your attention back to the original – and in comparison EM's delivery was less sharp, almost sheepish. Everyone just seemed ten years older (apart from Hannah Gordon, who hadn't aged at all). It was a dangerous route to take, and EM often told me that he hated going over old material, but there was little choice. So much material had been consumed in ten years of wonderful shows on the BBC, that there was very little left in the pot to scrape out. Ernie the playwright, the flat, the double bed, the guest star in front of the tabs, the skip-dancing off at the end – it was all great, but it was all very familiar. They needed new situations, but Thames weren't looking for new situations. They had bought into the huge success of *The Morecambe and Wise Show* that everyone had loved – and they just wanted more of the same.

chapter 12

EM wasn't the only one considering a future as an author. After the fiasco of the Cambridgeshire hotels, I'd had plenty of time to think about what I wanted to do with my life, and I kept coming back to an idea I'd had since I was sixteen, of earning a living by writing. But, as I was about to learn, it was difficult to become (and hopefully remain) a published writer and be the son of Eric Morecambe. The latter made the former nigh-on impossible. I mentioned this to EM once, and he was surprisingly understanding. He'd been a young lad who became Eric Morecambe; I was born Eric Morecambe's son. It was reassuring to know that he understood what a burden reflected fame can be, but it didn't simplify matters. Since his death I've achieved a balance between my aspirations as a writer and my status as EM's son. I've written nearly twenty books, worked on a West End play and a film and seen my career slowly develop. But, of all the stuff that I've published or worked on, the vast majority has been related in some way to the life and career of Eric Morecambe.

My first book was *Funnyman*, a collaboration with EM that brought together a lot of anecdotes and humorous lines in a gentle retelling of his life story. I wanted it to be a fun book, not scratching the surface too much: that's all I was capable of at the time, with EM still alive. I broached the idea to him during one of his visits to the hotel, after his heart attack – and he seemed interested, if not overwhelmingly enthusiastic, about it. I decided we should call it *Eric Through the Looking Glass*, which we both liked as a title, though neither of us was sure what, if anything, it meant. Our old friend Christopher Falkus at Eyre Methuen agreed to publish it, but changed the title to *Funnyman*.

I began sketching out ideas for chapters, and when Tracey and I decided to jack in our positions at the hotel I set up an office in a converted attic in Three Horseshoes Cottage and got to work. EM came to stay for a couple of nights in 1982, which was slightly uncomfortable at first – I don't think either of us could work out how to operate around each other in this unfamiliar menage. But he soon relaxed, and we had some fruitful discussions about the content and structure of the book. On the very first evening he came up with the idea that we should exchange letters that we would then publish at the conclusion of each chapter. 'Letters will give the whole thing a contemporary feel,' said EM.

The idea was contrived, but the letters were not – in fact they were great fun, because he wrote them very much in his comic persona.

Careless Rapture
C/o Captain Bloodless
Old Scotland Yard
Old Scotland

Dear Gary

As you can see, I went to Smith's and they refunded my money. I then bought the right typing paper. I think they thought I was a little crazy. One of the assistants told me what I should do with the old paper, but as I tried to explain, the paper was the wrong shape! He looked at me as if I had two heads. However!

I've been listening to the budget. Nothing ever seems to come down. The only thing that seems to come down with any certainty is my Y-fronts!

Re the book. Don't you think you've overdone the drinking? After all, if I had drunk the amount you seem to think I have, I would now be sitting on a park bench wondering where I could get my next glass of meths. My intake, at the most, was half a bottle of red wine, and in the evenings, two or maybe three scotches. I seem to be drunk or throwing a tantrum in every chapter. Say something pleasant about me. You know, something nice. There must have been one day...

Love
Dad

PS The next time you have a drink, remember I was strong enough to give it up.

I wasn't sure if he was striking a pose in anticipation of the book's publication, or making a definite defence against accusations I had supposedly made about his drinking. I've re-read the appropriate parts of the book, and firmly believe I did not overplay my observations in the least. He never really drank very much; he didn't have a strong constitution for alcohol. The wine and whisky he talks about certainly represented everday life – but he could binge when mixing with work-related company. That was where he could do himself no good, and it was less to do with his drinking than it was to do with an inability to resist temptation when it was there. Alcohol was not the problem; EM was the problem. He was an all-or-nothing sort of character. But never, in all those years, did I see him completely blotto. A bit woozy, perhaps; sleepy, hungover, but not roaring drunk. My remarks about his drinking touched a raw nerve; perhaps he recognized drink as a potential problem.

But when he decided to give up alcohol, he did it without any help. Never one to moderate, he just stopped. As you can tell, he was rather proud of that – because he'd certainly enjoyed a drink in earlier years. It wasn't so much about quantity with EM; it was the ritual that he enjoyed. He loved a dry martini, and about an hour before he wanted one he'd place a glass in the fridge to chill, occasionally returning to check on it. If it wasn't chilling enough, he'd place it in the freezer for 15 minutes. Then the martini would be lovingly poured over a bed of ice, and an olive dropped in to finish it off. Such preparation, such forethought.

In the seventies, when Eric and Ernie were touring theatres doing sell-out one-night stands, he would have a large whisky before going on stage. Ten years earlier, that would have been utterly out of the question. I suppose the success in the intervening years had made the difference; they were much more relaxed now.

Although he'd given up drink by 1982, EM did still smoke a pipe, and as a thank you for his support with my first book I bought him a new meerschaum pipe. He was pleased, and it was certainly a good deal from my point of view: EM had agreed not to take any of the royalties from *Funnyman*. There was a tobacconist in Cambridge I knew fairly well, and so I drove him there one morning to choose his thank-you present. EM had an unnerving habit of saying nothing when I was driving: I never fathomed whether it was because he didn't want to distract me, or whether he was frightened into silence – whatever the reasons, it made me feel like I was taking my test all over again.

We reached Cambridge and marched into the shop, much to the shock and pleasure of the man at the counter.

'It is you, isn't it?'

'Oh yes. At least it was the last time I looked. Now, young man, we've come to look at your pipes, if you'll pardon the expression.'

He began trying pipes like he was trying on glasses or an item of clothing. 'This one feels comfortable ... I like the shape of that one... This one has interesting features.' Half an hour later he had his pipe, neither of us knowing that he would give up smoking in six months' time. Never mind: it was what he wanted, and it mattered to me that I had made a gesture to acknowledge his generosity.

EM loved his pipes; he had a drawer filled with them in various states of disrepair, and a dozen or so of his favourites displayed on a shelf in his study. Five or six years earlier I'd bought him a Swiss pipe with a lid on the bowl to stop the ash blowing around; this appealed to his love of novelty items, and joined the other show specimens on the shelf, to be admired but never used. When I presented it to EM on his birthday he thanked me and left the room. Two minutes later he returned with his trousers tucked into his socks, Tyrolean fashion, and a trilby on his head. 'I'm just off to gather in the herd!'

Funnyman wasn't the only book EM was concerned with in 1982. He'd also written his first children's book, *The Reluctant Vampire*, which came out around the same time, also published by Eyre Methuen. There was a certain amount of cross-publicity from one book to the other, and there's a photo of the two of us together that could be used to sell both products. EM inscribed my copy: 'Isn't it sad to think that in twenty-five years you'll look like the fella with the cigar!'

EM wrote two vampire stories for children. *The Reluctant Vampire* was followed by *The Vampire's Revenge*, and he'd planned a third title, *The Vampire King*, which I completed after his death (although it was only ever published in Denmark). You can see from this extract from *The Vampire's Revenge* how confident his writing had become.

> He shaded his eyes as the sun dropped silently behind the distant hills; within seconds it was cool and dark, black dark, Vampire dark. Like all Vampires, he hated sunsets. Sunsets with that great, big, cruel ball of fire hanging in the sky, making the clouds a bright blue and red and pink and green and white and purple…'Horrible,' he thought.
>
> He had once heard about a thing called a rainbow, but, thank Dracula, he had never seen one. Who in their right minds would want to look at lots of colours in the shape of a large bow, hanging in the sky – not doing anything, just

hanging there. Now to see a falling star, that was something a bit special, because that meant in Vampire folklore that another Vampire had been born.

He left the cave and made his way to the dusty ribbon of the road, carrying his bent top hat, while, with his hands, he brushed away three years of dust from his suit.

EM and I did a certain amount of joint publicity for *Funnyman* and *The Reluctant Vampire*. We did a radio interview at Broadcasting House – my first time in a radio studio with EM, the first time our father–son relationship was placed on a professional footing, and it made me nervous. EM was robust and forthright, experience flowing from every pore. I was edgy and wary of what I was saying, especially as the show-business giant who just happened to be my father was also my subject – and was sitting right next to me.

The interviewer rather cheekily enquired if I'd one day write a more in-depth book about my father.

'Only after he's dead and gone,' I joked.

EM laughed. 'You can say what you like, when I'm dead and gone.'

He was right. *Funnyman* was written with EM breathing down my neck, and it was overwhelming in its blandness. Anecdote succeeded anecdote in a Dad-did-this, Dad-did-that manner, which I now feel uncomfortable about. It was a book by a young man with little experience. My parents quietly suggested at the time that it might be better to wait until I had more to say (and more freedom with which to say it?) – but I was twenty-five, and hungry to be published. While EM was alive, it was impossible to write honestly about him.

There was only one cloud on the horizon during the publication of *Funnyman*: EM and Ernie Wise had agreed to do another biography with the writer Michael Freedland, *There's No Answer to That*, and it was scheduled to come out at the same time. I tackled EM on the wisdom of this – and he was miffed with me for being miffed with him. 'It won't have any bearing on your book at all!' he said, but he was not the one to make such assurances. It was a poor decision that could only detract from both books.

•

I hadn't the faintest idea what to do after *Funnyman*. I'd set up my stall as Gary Morecambe, the son of Eric Morecambe – I'd chosen to use the Morecambe name for my publishing career after all, so any problems I encountered as the son of a famous man struggling to become an author were largely of my own making. The name would give me a foot in the door, but there was a limit as to how far that would take me. There are hundreds of celebrities trying to become authors; I had only a tiny little bit of reflected fame, and so the pressure was on to come up with the goods. And that pressure never goes away.

My second book was always going to be tricky. I wanted to write fiction, but I knew that the publisher would not share my enthusiasm. I attempted one or two novels which were truly abominable – even I recognized that. EM and I toyed with the idea of writing a novel together, but this was a non-starter. We half-seriously discussed writing a comedy crime caper set in Portugal – which we called *Figs!* – about a wealthy British comedian who had settled in the Algarve. It would include all those things that EM had encountered in

Portugal: the dodgy electricity and water supplies, the ex-pats, and so on. EM would do the funnies, I'd supply the narrative drive – but we failed to come up with a solid story to hang it all on, and nothing came of it. I was clutching at straws.

I had another story-line to put by him, the title for which was *Irving, The 13th Disciple!*.

EM loved the idea and the comic opportunities it gave rise to, but had difficulty over two issues. Firstly, he felt it would make a better TV sitcom than a novel, and secondly, he couldn't involve himself with something that was creating humour around a biblical setting. He felt that would hang badly with his image; his work in the past had always been locked in family entertainment: this would be a departure he felt uncomfortable about committing to. So we dropped it.

I was desperate to carry on writing, and I was in the lucky position of having a very substantial financial buffer in the shape of my parents. Without their support I would have abandoned the idea long ago, faced with the necessity of earning a living. Not that my parents had an open cheque book, but they were always sympathetic – and so, while I struggled to become a writer, I didn't have to miss too many meals.

At the time, the publication of *Funnyman* led only to anti-climax. By 1983 it had come and gone, and there was nothing issuing from my typewriter that was remotely publishable. I couldn't capitalize on my relationship with Eyre Methuen; *Funnyman* wasn't a book that automatically led to another book. The door that had been opened to me seemed to be closing fast.

The game was up in Cambridgeshire, and Tracey and I agreed that it was time for a complete rethink. We both loved

London, and decided to return to city life. We were too young to be isolated in the sticks like some semi-retired couple; Tracey could get a well-paid job in London (which she did, working for a property developer), and I could write and annoy every publisher on my doorstep (which I did). But I also needed a job. Through my years of working for Billy Marsh, I'd got to know Jack Breckon, head of publicity for Thames Television with offices off Euston Road. Jack was renowned for organizing the most outrageous stunts for a picture opportunity; Eric and Ernie were always worried that they'd appear on his hit-list.

Jack and a colleague, Roy Addison, let me know that a position was coming up with the animators Cosgrove and Hall, who made *Dangermouse* and *The Wind in the Willows* for Thames TV. With my funds depleted, and my writing career in a sorry state, I jumped at the opportunity. There were three rounds of interviews – but I didn't get the job.

Why didn't I work on my Dad to get me the job? It crossed my mind. A quick word from EM along the lines of 'We love doing *The Morecambe and Wise Show* for Thames, but there are lots of other broadcasters interested in us...and by the way, how's it going for Gary with that job he's after at Thames?' would assuredly have secured me the job. But he didn't suggest it, and I didn't ask him.

Even now I'm not sure how I feel about EM's stand-offish attitude to my career. Credit to him, he didn't beat about the bush. When we wrote *Funnyman*, he told me straight that he wouldn't use his reputation to pull any strings. I had a conversation with an editor at Eyre Methuen, who said, 'Of course, if your father insisted that we publish this novel you've sent us, we would have to consider it seriously.' I didn't run to tell EM that; I had some pride. It would have been bad enough getting through the back door in any case, but knowing that EM disapproved of that sort of thing would have made it worse. And what did I lose? Nothing really. The publisher might have run off 500 copies of the book just to please EM, the marketing budget would have been zero, and I would have looked pretty stupid.

I was used to living in my father's shadow; I had enjoyed it for much of the time. Did I need his help to get me that job at Thames? Perhaps I did. Perhaps I was too sensitive, too stupid to take advantage of the opportunities that were on offer. I'm not so slow off the blocks today, but now it's different: the shadow is still there, but he who casts it is not. The shadow that was once a negative influence in my life is now only a positive one. Of course, I paid a ludicrously high price for that; to attain my ends, my father had to die. I would rather have never published anything in my life if it could have kept EM alive, but I'd be lying if I said that I haven't enjoyed the opportunities that his name has brought me.

So I remained unemployed. Luckily for me, Tracey had her finger on the pulse of property and realized that the flat in which we'd been living for six months had increased in value by a colossal amount. The property boom of the eighties was well under way, and we were in the right place at the right time to get a useful slice of the action. I had, through good luck, discovered a way in which to support my career as a writer.

For the next two years we did rather well, but things were about to change forever. EM was in the final year of his life.

chapter 13

In retrospect I can see that EM's life was winding down from 1982 to 1984. He'd fallen out of love with Portugal; many of the things he'd found charming in the sixties and seventies just got on his nerves now. He bought a condominium in Palm Beach, Florida, in 1982 – it was an impulse purchase. 'As soon as he saw it,' my mother said, 'that was it. Instantly, he had to buy it.' It had its own security man, its own air-conditioning, and buttons to communicate with both. It was a much easier way of life than Portugal, and I think EM was finally allowing himself a little bit of luxury at the end of his days.

Tracey and I joined EM and Joan for a holiday in Palm Beach in October 1982, little knowing that this would be our last holiday abroad together. We were greeted at Miami airport by a Pan Am rep who, on seeing that Tracey wore glasses, immediately shook her by the hand and said, 'I'm a great fan of your father's!'

'Wrong person,' said Tracey, nodding towards me.

The condo was great if you like condos. EM loved to tinker with the air-con, turning it up so high that you could see your own breath in the room. In the basement there was table tennis, where my mother embarrassingly thrashed me. The uniformed security guard was always there with a smile

on his face. Tracey and I were the youngest people in the
place by about four decades.

The local restaurants served bountiful, limitless amounts
of food. And there were wonderful attractions in the area: we
visited Disney World for a few days, a demanding schedule,
but EM insisted he was up to it. There was a very tall, fake
tree at Disney World which I felt we should climb, mainly as
it didn't have any queues – and we soon discovered why. At
the top we entered a room where two puppets were sharing
corny conversation like some appalling double act. EM shook
his head and sighed; he was tired and out of breath. 'You've
brought me all the way up here to see *The Two Ronnies*?'

His attitude to his writing career also became a little shaky
in the last year of his life. I've said he enjoyed writing books
and it's true – he loved going out to lunch with publishers
and talking about projects, and he loved seeing the finished
product. But he was realistic about his writing; he often said,
'I wouldn't even get published if it wasn't for the Morecambe
name.' He understood the limitations of his talent, but he
could still get huffy when it was pointed out to him. He
embarked on a series of magazine articles about various
subjects such as dieting – and I agreed to edit them for him.
My father was my greatest hero – still is – but I'd be lying if I
said I didn't take a great deal of reassurance from the fact he
couldn't write articles with any skill. All of them were
rejected, much to his fury. 'I'm too old to do auditions!' he'd
say – but the articles were really bad. They read like a script
for a bad British sitcom, with no understanding of the people
he was writing for. In the diet article, the reader is supposed
to be considering a menu in a contemporary English pub, but

the dialogue is post Second World War: 'Ooh, that sounds a bit rum, dearie!'

I was horrified, and I didn't have a clue how to tell him how bad these pieces were. There was only one article that was good enough – and that was about Des O'Connor. The editor wanted to publish it, and indeed paid EM for it, but felt that it showed Des in such a dodgy light that they couldn't run it without getting into trouble.

There were these little hints in 1982 and 1983 that all wasn't going as well for EM as it might have done – not to mention the fact that the shows they were doing for Thames weren't really up to scratch. But EM was only fifty-six or fifty-seven at the time – we had no idea that he was so close to the end of his working life, the end of his life, period. As usual we saw the signs only in retrospect. By and large EM was enjoying himself, enjoying his work, and reaping the rewards of a phenomenally successful career.

Unlike a lot of entertainers that I've met or read about, EM never really felt that there was a downside to fame. Sometimes he got irritated by the public recognition, but even then he was normally polite and friendly, despite the incredible rudeness of some people. A man came up to us once in an airport and said, 'Are you in disguise, mate?'

'No. Are you?'

And at the same airport a woman said, 'You look just like Eric Morecambe. I bet you wish you had his money!' EM just laughed and agreed with her. Again at the airport, a group of twenty-somethings surrounded EM with bits of paper and not a pen in sight. He'd only come to pick me up, and the airport was sweltering.

'Sign this, Eric!'

'How about a please, please?'

'Oh yeah. Please sign it, Eric.'

'That's better. Good manners never hurt, you know...'

It's the only time I can remember him being testy with an autograph hunter; usually he'd put up with any nonsense, sign his name and crack a few jokes. But by now he was tired, and his patience was running a bit low.

He would never complain about any of this, though: he hated 'moaners', as he called them. He saw only the positive aspects of his success: the money and the acclaim, the opportunity to give his wife and children creature comforts and financial support whenever they needed it. His twitchy temperament made it impossible for him to be a truly responsible parent, but he wasn't an irresponsible one.

He believed that fame was there to be enjoyed; it was our duty, he felt, to make the most of it, because one day it might disappear.

'But Dad,' I'd moan, 'I don't want to go to the Grosvenor House Hotel tonight and meet Elton John and everyone.'

'You'll regret it one day, when the invitations stop!'

I don't think EM expected constant gratitude, but it would have grated enormously if we'd made a fuss about any of the opportunities his fame had given us. Fame had given us financial stability for life, and while he never rubbed our noses in the fact he certainly didn't want us to kick against it. He never expected us to embrace show business; as I've said before, Gail, Steven and I were kept pretty separate from that side of his life. Our upbringing was stiflingly normal, with moments of great excitement and glamour thrown in.

EM was very level-headed about his fame, particularly with regard to the press. His favourite pearl of wisdom on the subject was: 'You never want to believe how good the papers say you are – and you never want to believe how bad they say you are. The truth is somewhere between the two.' He'd also say: 'Whatever hurtful things the papers might write, just remember that it's only tomorrow's fish-and-chip wrapping.' He drew strength from this, and it kept his feet on the ground. One of his great qualities was his modesty. If he examined himself – which he did rarely, believing that self-analysis would destroy the spontaneity of his work – he concluded that he had just been in the right place at the right time. Even when he was awarded the OBE in 1976, he said, 'All this fuss, and I'm only a clown.'

I remember a man coming up to him in the street and saying, 'I saw you on telly the other night, Eric.'

'I hope we're still friends,' was the reply.

He downplayed his fame and success, but he loved receiving his OBE. He was a big fan of the royal family, and he was thrilled to learn that they were fans of Morecambe and Wise. He enjoyed the accolades, but they never made him big headed.

By the eighties, EM was a sort of elder statesman of British comedy. Everyone, even the young generation of 'alternative' comedians who were breaking through, acknowledged him as the master. And EM was always very generous with advice and support to young comedians. Lenny Henry recalls how, as a teenager, he was working on a show way down the bill from Morecambe and Wise. He was having a tough time of it, particularly from the other comedians, and when he ran over his allocated nine minutes he got a real grilling from the management. Feeling guilty, he went to see Eric and Ernie to apologize.

'It doesn't matter to us,' said Eric. 'But next time, go on and do the same thing, and just tell them you'll drop the shoe routine.'

'But I don't do a shoe routine,' said a confused Lenny.

'Exactly,' said Eric. 'But they won't know that.'

And it worked: next time Lenny went on he said to the managers, 'Don't worry, fellas, I've dropped the shoe routine.' He did a full eleven minutes and nobody said a word.

I met Richard Curtis and Rowan Atkinson at my parents' house in the late seventies. They were both at Oxford, and we knew them because my childhood friend Bill Drysdale was sharing a house with Rowan on Woodstock Road. Even back then Richard and Rowan were working on comedy together, with Richard as the straight man to Rowan's clown. Quite a bit of Mr Bean was there in embryonic form even in those long-ago days. EM invited them to the house one evening, and they spent hours talking about comedy. I know it was a big thrill for them to meet EM – and he got enormous pleasure from watching the burgeoning career of these two talented young men over the next five years.

•

By 1983 the deterioration in Morecambe and Wise's work for Thames was becoming painfully apparent. The Christmas show (which didn't go out until Boxing Day, because Christmas Day was on a Sunday, when LWT had control of the schedules) was their poorest ever; by now they were even recycling material written by Hills and Green from their original ATV shows. Those closest to EM felt it, and the public felt it too. I think EM also knew it, but he wasn't best placed to criticize his own work. When you work on something so constantly, and you have such high standards, and you've been fighting progressive heart disease, and you're toying with other interests, it's easier to say, 'The show wasn't that bad though, was it?' – which is exactly what he did say. 'Not bad at all,' chorused the response.

Even worse was the film that Morecambe and Wise had made for Euston Films – part of the deal that had lured them over to Thames from the BBC. *Night Train to Murder* was a disaster. EM knew it too. After a screening in early 1984, he said, 'It's awful. Not what we set out to make at all.' He insisted that the film should somehow be 'lost' in the scheduling, and it was. It was finally transmitted in a children's afternoon slot after EM's death.

On Christmas Day, when EM and I were sitting at the table drinking port, he said, 'I want to ask you a question.' What's this, I wondered, suspicious of the formal tone he was introducing.

'I'm thinking of retiring,' he said. 'What do you reckon?'

Well, he'd finally got round to asking me. He'd been putting the question in a less direct fashion to my mother, to Ernie, to Gail, for some months.

'The decision has to be yours, Dad.'

Ernie was part of the problem. EM didn't want to let him down – and Ernie was still as fit as a fiddle, with plenty more working years left in him. Making any decision that would put an end to Ernie's career would be very hard for EM. It was one thing to stop his own career – quite another to stop someone else's.

EM nodded sagely. 'It's taking too much out of me. I want to do other things, not just the funnies all the time. I'm not sure I even enjoy watching comedy any more, let alone performing it.' After decades of comedy, was his belief in humour as a way to validate his existence finally beginning to wane? It must get hard to wake up every morning wanting to be funny – especially when, as in EM's case, reality is distinctly lacking in funniness. His health wasn't good. During a Keystone Kops sequence for the show, EM threw himself against a wall, as written in the script, and put his heart out of rhythm, necessitating another trip to the hospital.

'You could cut back,' I said. 'Just do one-off specials.'

It was an idea he was toying with. He was looking forward to 'reclaiming' Christmas night in 1984; the fact he'd been shunted to Boxing Day contributed to his thoughtful mood that night.

Whatever the reactions to the 1983 Christmas show, EM started 1984 full of plans and clearly in no mood to retire. His diary was crammed – too crammed, as everyone wanted a piece of him. But he found time to relax with my mother, too: it was a taste of what semi-retirement would be like. EM could have had a nice life if he had retired from the show: he could have written books, done personal appearances and panel games, and spent plenty of time fishing. It should have been a pleasant time in his life, but instead his failing health began to cast a deeper shadow.

He had a stomach and chest complaint which he assumed was nothing more serious than trapped wind; he was

PREVIOUS PAGE From 1975 onwards, EM and EW would concentrate more and more on musical routines, both men fascinated by the Hollywood legends of yesteryear such as Astaire, Kelly and Rogers.

TOP Eric and Ernie's bed routine; breaking boundaries without ever referring to them.

ABOVE LEFT The early days, the song, smile and gag style of entertaining – the origins of the modern Morecambe and Wise act.

ABOVE RIGHT A classic scene from a Morecambe and Wise Christmas show, one in which Bruce Forsyth memorably guested as Father Christmas.

ABOVE LEFT A famously low-budget BBC publicity shot announcing the arrival of EM and EW at the Beeb.

ABOVE RIGHT EM was never one to miss a gag opportunity. Hyde Park and Wise on set.

BELOW Robin Day guests on the show, considered by him to be one of the highlights of his career.

OPPOSITE PAGE, TOP LEFT EM and EW with the beautiful Kate O'Mara.

TOP RIGHT EM promoting Luton at any given opportunity.

CENTRE Among others, Michael Aspel (top row, first left), Barry Norman (top row, third left), Frank Bough (to right of Barry) and Richard Baker (top row, second from right) in an unrehearsed dance routine that EM was convinced would never work.

BOTTOM LEFT Early days at the BBC. EM on the comeback trail very soon after his first heart attack.

BOTTOM RIGHT EM and EW with Angela Rippon.

ABOVE Diana Rigg with EM, who she recently described as one of the sexiest men she ever met!

LEFT Glenda Jackson and EM. Glenda had such belief in Morecambe and Wise that she was the first superstar to risk her reputation by appearing on the show.

TOP Des O'Connor appears with EM and EW and finally gets his revenge.

ABOVE EM loved to receive awards, and when he didn't, he wasn't against handing them out to himself anyway!

OVERLEAF André Preview, Previtt, Previn playing all the right notes for EM and EW. Possibly the highest point of their illustrious careers.

reluctant to go to a doctor, fearing, I suppose, that he'd hear bad news. He got on with life and hoped the pain would go away, but it didn't. Eventually Joan took him to see a doctor, who suspected a possible hiatus hernia and fixed a date for an X-ray. The results came back negative. EM had a visit from a heart specialist as a matter of course; pills were prescribed, and he felt better immediately. His heart was slightly enlarged, but he seemed fit enough.

At this time EM's character changed. He began tidying his office, dealing with outstanding paperwork, giving everyone odds and sods like old pipes, books and so forth. Temperamentally he altered, too: he was easily upset, and became unusually sensitive to comments in the press. He read some quotes in one of the tabloids that were attributed to Ernie and was deeply distressed. Ernie assured him that the quotes had not come from him, and really there was nothing to get that upset about – but for some reason it really affected EM. And this was a man who had put up with press intrusion all his life, even taking calls when they phoned him for a quote in the middle of Sunday lunch – as they frequently did.

At a function EM started having a go at a reporter from the paper who had printed the article. It was so unlike him – and deeply concerning for his family. He normally made a joke out of this type of thing; there's a wonderful line in one *Morecambe and Wise Show* when Eric turns to Ernie and says, 'Go and get the papers and see if we've split up again.'

He became almost cantankerous on the subject of success. Shortly before he died EM, my mother and I were chatting in their TV room, and he started to talk about the big money-earners. He mentioned Andrew Lloyd Webber. I said, 'Well, at least he's wealthy enough to choose what he wants to do. Art for art's sake.'

'Don't be ridiculous,' snapped EM. 'You can never have enough! He works for the money!'

This surprised me: EM had always said he enjoyed entertaining people for the sheer pleasure of making people laugh. He used to say that he only enjoyed show business once he was a star and started making money, but that can't have been entirely true: how else would he have sustained himself during twenty years on the road, if all it came down to was money in the bank? Money was important to him, as was recognition, but it wasn't the sole basis of his career.

My last meeting in public with EM was at the Royal Gardens Hotel in Kensington. Tracey and I had settled in town, and it was easy for us to nip over to meet up with him whenever he was attending a function. I got on very well with my father at this time: he was slower and easier, worn down by a mixture of continual comedy and continual illness. I can't remember what brought him into town that day, but I know that I was very busy and I turned up at the hotel in jeans and trainers. If I hadn't been a guest of EM, I don't think I would have been allowed in.

EM grimaced. 'Do you always look so smart when you go out?'

'Sorry about that,' I said. 'I didn't have time to change.'

'Or shave.'

Despite his fluctuating mood during this period, he was on good form that afternoon. We ordered tea and listened to the piano, which was always a great source of amusement to

EM. Once in Portugal we'd been listening to a very average hotel pianist when EM turned to me and said 'Ask him if he knows the "A" train. If he says yes, tell him it leaves in five minutes!'

In May 1984 I spent a couple of nights at my parents' house, and I could sense that EM was worried about my chosen career and my future. I was entering a profession with no guaranteed salary, no perks, no pension. It's a make-or-break career, like the one he'd chosen, and he felt it was unlikely that lightning would strike in the same family twice.

Mid-morning on Sunday 26 May I said goodbye to my father for the last time. He gave me a big hug, which was unusually tactile for him. He seemed a bit confused, and was concerned that Tracey and I had plans that took us elsewhere. He and Joan were going up to Tewkesbury, where he was booked in to a theatre to be interviewed in front of a live audience.

We couldn't know that this would be the last parting between us. No more gags, no more laughs, no more flippant asides and comic interruptions to our daily life.

The Tewkesbury show turned out to be EM's last performance. There was no Ernie Wise. EM was interviewed by Stan Stennett, who had worked with Morecambe and Wise in many a summer season and panto in the fifties. EM was relaxed; sitting in front of 800 people and talking about his life was not a stressful concept. Despite a few health scares in the previous weeks, he was looking forward to it.

EM spoke fluently and revealingly on stage that Sunday night, joined in with the band at the end, walked off to a standing ovation, then collapsed and died.

In the early hours of the morning my mother rang to tell me that EM was dead. As I lay back in bed, stunned, I had an unworthy image of him being rushed from Tewkesbury to Cheltenham Hospital in the ambulance and saying his last words to the medical team around him: 'He's not going to sell much ice-cream going at that speed!'

When my mother returned the following day, among the bits and pieces that accompanied her were EM's glasses. How shockingly poignant it was to see this item – this prop – away from the famous face they had adorned for years. A little while later I read a Len Deighton novel, in which he describes so well how personal glasses are in terms of their owner: 'If there's anything more pathetic than a dead man's dog, it's a dead man's spectacles. Every bend and shine belonged to its wearer and to no one else, nor would ever.'

Life is transitory. It mattered not that EM was loved and cherished by countless millions. He had publicly reviewed his life and career in front of eight hundred people, and concluded his remarkable story.

The days and weeks following EM's death sped by, yet there was a sense of time standing still; it was like being in the centre of a vortex. We guarded against the 'if onlys' – if only he'd rested more, if only he'd not gone to Tewkesbury that night. A doctor told us that he could still have died that very night just getting up to turn the TV off, which was a great comfort.

The funeral was a big affair, with literally thousands of mourners. The line began a few yards from my parents' house and snaked all the way to Harpenden church: a distance of about three miles.

During those first weeks there was a sense that it had all been an elaborate gag, that EM could step through the door at any moment and say, 'Evening, all. Sorry I'm late, but I've been irrigating the desert. Not easy on your own!'

But EM made no return, and we remained cocooned inside our fortress at Harpenden, with journalists and photographers hovering outside the door, awaiting any opportunity to attack. I went on to automatic pilot, switching into the publicity mode I'd learnt at Billy Marsh's. I fielded calls and callers, organized current projects and tried to keep our lives on some kind of sane track.

When there was no longer any need to stay around for my mother's sake, Tracey and I decided to leave the Harpenden home and return to our life in London. Summer had come and gone and the general hubbub surrounding EM's passing was ebbing away. Only then, as we were about to leave, did I crack. It was as if someone had told me for the first time that my father had died. I spent an hour in the cloakroom, weeping inconsolably. My father, the man of a million quips and innocent mischief, had gone for good. It was the same cloakroom EM had taken to using after his first heart attack, unable to climb the stairs. There was a worn patch of carpet outside where many great Subbuteo matches had taken place. These memories were like stab wounds of what once had been and could never be again. You can only be stiff-upper-lipped for a while; grief will overwhelm you at some point.

I kept noticing little things, like Luton Town scores flickering on the TV. 'Dad would have been pleased with that result...'

chapter 14

The death of my father was the start of a long process of coming to terms with the effect he had on my life. Up to the age of twenty-eight I'd lived entirely in the shadow of a famous man; sometimes I loved it, sometimes I hated it, but I could never evaluate it because I had never known any different. With EM's death came a chance to look back at our relationship with a growing degree of objectivity.

One of the hardest aspects of being Eric Morecambe's son was the comparison between his achievements and my achievements. Every time I celebrated a birthday in my twenties and thirties, I'd compare myself to EM at that age. When he was thirty-two, Morecambe and Wise were conquering Australia. At thirty-five, *The Morecambe and Wise Show* was screening on ATV to increasing success. At forty-two, they moved to the BBC and their historic career began in earnest – and EM had his first heart attack. After the age of forty-two I stopped comparing. It's pointless, and it's discouraging. I had never been in competition with EM, so it was time to stop the comparisons and get on with my own existence.

If you look at it from another angle, of course, EM died at fifty-eight, and I hope to go on for a good deal longer. Fifty-eight sounds terribly young to me now; it's the age I'll reach in 2014.

Rather than comparing what we've all achieved, I've tried to look back on how having EM as a father affected Gail's life, Steven's life and my life.

Gail believes that she lacked self-esteem in her early life; it wasn't until her mid-twenties that she realized she had some value in her own right, and not just as EM's daughter. Even today she has those lingering doubts in the back of her mind. Perhaps this stems from the fact that we were instructed at a very young age to modify our behaviour so that it reflected well on EM; we came to think that we existed only as reflections of our parents, and only did well when they said we did well. This is true of all children, but I think it's amplified in the case of the children of the famous, because the levels of expectation are much higher, and the amount of attention you're likely to get from complete strangers is greatly increased.

Gail avoided telling people what EM did for a living; in fact, she went to great lengths to delay anyone finding out. As soon as people knew who her father was, the conversation immediately changed: 'What's he like at home? What's it like seeing him on telly? Does he really like Ernie? What famous people have you met? You're not a bit how I imagined you to be!' Did these people really lie in bed at night wondering what Eric Morecambe's daughter was like? It got to the point where Gail began to think that people were only interested in her because of who her father was.

EM didn't always help. Gail, like me, was quite shy as a teenager, and to make matters worse she had her fair share of spots. She always did a good job of concealing them with make-up, but EM delighted in pointing this out. She could enter a room full of adults, start shaking hands and smiling at complete strangers, friends of Dad's, then he'd come up and say, 'You've done a good job covering up those spots, Gail!' I don't know why he'd say something like that: perhaps it was just to get a laugh, perhaps it was to knock us back and make sure we didn't get too big headed. I don't think it was deliberately cruel, but things like that can really hurt teenagers. Mind you, he was just as likely to come up to you at any time, put an arm round you and say, 'You do know that I love you, don't you?'

Gail sang in a choir from the age of eight, but EM never went to hear her sing. In 1984 she was due to perform Elgar's *The Dream of Gerontius* at Ely Cathedral, and to her astonishment EM said he'd like to go with Joan to hear her. He died a few weeks before the performance. Joan went, which was brave when you consider that *The Dream of Gerontius* is about the journey of a man's soul at the moment of his death.

When she was young, Gail had some interest in going on the stage or singing or modelling for a living, but she got no encouragement from our parents and soon abandoned the idea. That's when she decided to become a nursery nurse – and it was absolutely the right career for her. Only recently has she given up working with children. Now she runs her own greetings card company, known as Morecambe Moments. One of her ranges is called Celebriteds, which features a teddy bear doing impressions of famous people. EM was the first in the range, of course.

Though fully embraced by the Morecambe family, Steven was only fourteen when EM died, and so he hadn't yet embarked on adult life. He ran a bit wild after EM's death, no longer having a male authority figure in his life, and he started to get into trouble. Nothing serious – he just started going out with friends and not telling his mother when he'd be home, which was sometimes days later. For a while he worked in the funeral trade, then he drove lorries – which I'm sure isn't what EM envisaged him doing for a living! EM had always admired Steven's sturdy build and had quiet hopes that he would transform into a fine opening batsman – EM adored cricket. He always made it plain to Steven that he was one of three children and that it wasn't a case of having two children and then later an adopted one.

When Steven lost his HGV licence after a drink-driving offence, he told me that EM would have knocked him for six if he'd found out. Steven moved to Australia for two years; when he returned to England he moved back in with his mother, which was hard for both of them. By that time the ban had passed, he got his HGV licence back and moved into his own house in Harpenden, which was better for everyone concerned.

'Even now,' says Steven, 'I have really bad bouts of missing Dad. Whenever I'm depressed, I go down to the graveyard where his ashes are to have a chat with him. One night I drove all the way to Morecambe to be beside his statue. I resent the fact that he died so early in my life; there were too many things left unsaid. If I could see him one more time, I'd ask him if he was proud of me, the way I've turned out, despite everything. He'd probably tell me I'm rubbish, but then we're all looking for a bit of approval. That never goes away.'

As for my own life, I've spent the last twenty years since EM's death trying to work out exactly what he's meant to me. During his lifetime I felt overshadowed by him, in awe of him, even crushed by him. After his death, once I'd adjusted to his absence, I began to realize that he was still the most important thing in my life – and in some ways the best thing in my life.

In 1984 and 1985 I tried to get my writing career back on track, but it was too early. I'd written a few celebrity features on people like Judi Dench and Nanette Newman, which I was hoping to sell to magazines as a freelance contributor, but I didn't have the heart to start flogging them. How would it have looked to any editor I approached? 'Gary Morecambe's just lost his father, and here he is asking if I'd publish a personality interview he's done.'

Then, when Tracey and I had returned to London and she was back at work in the property business, I picked up a pile of notes from EM's office headed 'Stella: a novel by Eric Morecambe'. The handwriting was nearly illegible, but gradually I began to piece it together, and I realized that this was a nearly complete book. With a little bit of care it could be turned into a publishable work. I set about finishing it off, which was a strange experience for me. There was no disguising EM as the author of the book, but he'd taken a major step forward in balancing the comedian he was with the author he hoped to develop into – as you can see in this extract. The character Sadie – EM's mother in name only – is dying of cancer, but she and her husband Tommy don't know it yet.

Tommy cut through a piece of Stella's home-baked fruit cake. It made as much impression as a spoon on a piece of solid oak. 'Think this cake'll have to be chucked,' he shouted to her from the kitchen. She came in.

'Don't waste it. Give it to the birds.'

'The poor sods'll never take off again if they eat this.'

'No swearing, Tommy Moran,' she scolded.

'Sorry,' he said insincerely. He didn't mean to sound insincere, but it had grown that way, because he was always apologizing. 'I'll get something else we can nibble at with our cuppa.'

'I'm not hungry, pet,' she told him.

'You're never hungry, these days,' he commented. Tommy had been worried about her for some time now. She hadn't been eating properly for months. At first he thought it was due to her upset over Stella – the way she had virtually ignored them when they'd taken all the trouble and expense to go and see her in Manchester – but now he wasn't so sure. She was very thin, whatever the cause. Maybe it was his own fault. Most things were his fault, or so Sadie told him. Maybe he shouldn't have made such a big fuss over giving up the three-piece suite in favour of seeing Stella's show. Thinking back, he had gone on about it quite a bit, especially when it had turned into such a disappointing reunion.

As if hearing his thoughts, she said, 'I wish I was still working with Stella.'

It sounds fanciful to say that I felt EM's presence at every moment I worked on the book, but I truly did. At the funny lines I could hear him chuckle. At the poignant moments he was gently nodding his head, delighted at the new areas his writing was beginning to go in. He was a bright man, despite the paucity of his education, and surprisingly well read, as if desperate to remedy his childhood academic inadequacies. Given time, he would have been publishing astonishingly literate material for a man of such humble origins.

Stella was published in 1985 by Severn House, and I launched myself on to the publicity circuit to promote it. One of my dates was in Morecambe – my first visit there for a number of years. After the book-signing session in Lancaster, I took myself off for a trip down memory lane. The promenade, the houses in which my grandparents had lived, the terraced house in which EM had been born, were all still there – sixty years of history compressed into one hour.

•

In 1987 Tracey and I took an extended holiday in Asia. I hadn't really had a break since EM's death three years previously, and all the trauma and ballyhoo that surrounded his passing – but this was more than just a holiday. It was one of the best experiences of my life. We went to Cairo, then to Bombay and Thailand. I couldn't have been further away from Morecambe and Wise – or so I thought. On the virtually deserted beach of Koh Samui in southern Thailand, a fellow traveller was talking about the homeland. We got on to the subject of golf, I don't know why, and he talked about a course he enjoyed playing. It was the course just behind my parents' house.

'I know that course,' I said.

'Really? Have you played it?'

'Once or twice. Actually, I used to live near it.'

'You probably lived near Eric Morecambe, then. Did you know that?'

Cue explanation and invariable shock.

On a return visit to Bangkok I fell ill with flu and lay shivering in a hotel bedroom for a few days. Like most hotels it had a film channel, and I sat watching some Charles Bronson movie. The film ended, but the video remained playing to reveal what had been taped over: EM's funeral. Suddenly, on the other side of the world in a strange bed with a raging temperature, I was reliving my own father's funeral.

In a back street in Delhi I saw a second-hand bookshop – something I can never resist. There, in an unkempt pile, in between a book on the inhabitants of the Himalayan foothills and an Indian recipe book, was one of EM's children's stories. Of course I had to buy it. How did it get there? I wondered. It must have been bought in England, read somewhere in Asia, and wound up in Delhi. Then it came home with me, to complete the circle.

When we came back to England I started working with another writer called Martin Sterling, who was introduced to me by my agent, Andrew Lownie. Martin, like me, is a big fan of James Bond, and we decided we should write a biography of Timothy Dalton, who had just taken over the role from Roger Moore. We immediately ran into problems. Both of us were new to biography and were far too keen to seek the approval of our subject matter. A few chapters did the rounds of the publishers, and we had a brief bite from one, whose initial interest was soon modified with too many provisos. Soon after that the project disappeared – and so did I.

Inspired by Peter Mayles' best seller *A Year in Provence*, Tracey and I decided to move to France. Our first child, Jack, had just been born, premature and weighing only 2½ lbs, but, thanks to the children's special unit at Queen Charlotte's Hospital, a healthy baby and a bouncing toddler. The three of us moved to Brittany at the end of 1988.

I needed a break from Morecambe and Wise. In 1988 the public's attitude was still one of great sadness that Eric had died so young; it had yet to change to the fondness and celebration that came about in the nineties. I wanted to be somewhere where people might say, 'Morecambe and Who?'

Perhaps Brittany wasn't the ideal spot for a two-year sabbatical; for one thing, the weather is too similar to Britain's, and the property we bought near the medieval town of Dinan was a wreck. But the first summer was a blur of wine and cider, eating *galettes* and going for long bike rides. We spent whole days on the beach with Jack and then, the following year, with his brother Henry, who was born at St Malo hospital on the coast.

For the first six months we deliberately avoided having a television or a video, and to begin with we didn't miss them at all. But then the winter arrived, and it was damp, quiet, isolated and often painfully lonely. So we bought a TV and a video and we unpacked all our tapes – including *The Morecambe and Wise Shows* – from their cartons.

I joined the Dinan Table Ronde and made a lot of French friends, among them the man who had arranged our house and car insurance in Brittany, Alain Montagnon. He was fascinated by the idea that I had a famous father of whom he had never heard, and I could always see doubt in his eyes.

One day in his office he beamed at me and shook my hand with extra fervour.

'It's true!' he said.

'What's true?'

'Your father is famous!'

'Yes, I know that. But how did you find out?'

'Ah,' he said, looking rather pleased with himself, 'I had some English clients in the office the other day, and I told them that we knew the son of Eric Morecambe. Well, I didn't expect a reaction.'

'And what was the reaction?'

'They couldn't believe it! They were amazed! So your father really is famous!'

In 1991 we returned to England. Living in France and trying to be a writer wasn't going to work out; I could either stay there and not write, or come back to England and get back into the swing of things. We kept a flat in London, which we let out, but settled in the Wiltshire/Dorset/Somerset borders. Our third son, Arthur, was born in December.

My attitude to Morecambe and Wise had changed. By 1991 they were still highly regarded but quietly forgotten. I didn't want it to stay that way. In a complete turnabout of my attitude prior to departing for France, I had an overwhelming urge to remind everyone just what Morecambe and Wise stood for in British entertainment history.

Only months before we decided to come home Martin Sterling contacted me with an idea for a stage play about Morecambe and Wise. He'd sent me the outline of a script which we could develop together, if I thought the idea was sound.

And that was the first inkling of an idea that was to preoccupy me for the following ten years.

chapter 15

The plan to write a play about Morecambe and Wise kicked around for the next three years, while Martin Sterling and I wrote a book about them, *Behind the Sunshine*, which was published in 1994. It sold very well that summer and was a clear indicator that there was a groundswell of interest in Morecambe and Wise ten years after EM's death.

Early in 1994 I got a call from Jan Kennedy, Billy Marsh's successor as EM's agent, who told me that the West End producer David Pugh was interested in staging a play about the lives of Morecambe and Wise and wanted to meet me. David was totally enthusiastic, and totally honest about the fact that he didn't have the faintest idea how a stage tribute could be done. We met up in Bournemouth for a brainstorming weekend, armed to the teeth with Morecambe and Wise videos; by coincidence my bedroom overlooked the Pavilion Theatre where Eric and Ernie had made many appearances. But no inspiration was forthcoming; no glimmer of an idea that went beyond the obvious.

Back in London we met up with Arthur Smith (*An Evening with Gary Lineker*), Ned Sherrin, Robert Lindsay and many others to discuss the play: it was all most enjoyable, but nothing came of it. Martin and I quite liked the obvious route

– a direct impression of Eric and Ernie in which their story unfolds. This was anathema to David Pugh – and thankfully he wouldn't budge. He knew it would be impossible to impersonate the original with any degree of success.

We talked to directors who wanted to cast stars – Russ Abbot and Michael Williams – as Eric and Ernie. We talked to Ernest Maxin, producer of many of the BBC shows, who wanted to direct a 'biopic' of Morecambe and Wise's life – a biopic for the stage, that is. Martin and I produced a script, but we weren't happy with it. Other directors came and went, but things always fell apart when it came to the question of who would play Eric and Ernie. We worked with David Benson for a while; he'd done a very successful show based on the life of Kenneth Williams, which was as much about David's life as it was about Williams's. That should have given me a clue, but I was still way off the mark.

By this time I was so weary of the whole notion of the project that I was beginning to lose faith in it, but we'd already generated a considerable amount of media interest. I went on Richard and Judy's television show in Manchester, and did a lengthy interview for the *Sunday Times* and the *Mail*, which generated a great deal of attention and should have been enough to kickstart the project. So when we had nothing to follow it up with, we looked foolish. I should have kept my mouth shut until we had something ready.

Quite early on Martin and I had secured the interest of Ernie Wise. At first he was uncertain: 'I suppose this sort of thing is inevitable,' he said. But as time went on Ernie grew keener and we had a couple of meetings to discuss what we might do. Then Ernie had a stroke, and his enthusiasm for the play waned. I saw him at Billy Marsh's memorial service in 1996 and he told me he'd prefer it if a play about Morecambe and Wise was shelved to a later date, adding, 'You can do what you like when I'm dead and gone' – just as EM had said.

I don't know how serious Ernie was about this, but his comments certainly curtailed my enthusiasm. For some years the idea went on virtual, if not complete, hold.

In the meantime, there was a considerable increase of interest in Morecambe and Wise. Our book, *Behind the Sunshine*, was doing well, and coincided with a television retro on the double act in the summer of 1994, designed to tie-in with the tenth anniversary of EM's passing. Orchestrated by Alan Yentob, they broadcast an initial three shows introduced by comedian/writer Ben Elton. The viewing figures were excellent, almost staggering, so three more were at once commissioned. It was like old times again. The country was reawakening to the sound of 'Bring Me Sunshine', and I could operate with a freedom denied me previously.

The Morecambe and Wise revival gathered pace over the next few years. In 1996, to celebrate sixty years of BBC television, there was an awards programme in which the BBC gave out 'Aunties' to the winners voted for by the public. Morecambe and Wise won both their categories – best comedians of all time, best light entertainment programme of all time. In 1998 a *Radio Times* poll voted them the best TV comedy stars of all time, and an internet poll the same year voted EM the best British comic of the twentieth century.

Around Christmas time 1998 BBC1 screened an *Omnibus* film, *The Heart and Soul of Eric Morecambe*. I'd approached a producer, Anthony Haas, with the idea of some kind of special on EM, and he brought in Watchmaker Productions to work on the show. I had mixed feelings about the final results. It was very glossy and cinematic, but it seemed too arty-farty for the simplicity of EM's nature, all hazy shots, close-ups, strange establishing shots. Much of the running time concentrated on EM's ill health, which gave an unjust slant to what he always acknowledged had been a wonderful life. Many viewers felt that EM had been a victim of comedy – that his need to entertain people had finally killed him. But his story is much bigger than that, and much happier than that, and I felt perturbed that viewers might look upon it in that light.

The revival continued to gather momentum. In 1999 came the BAFTA fellowship award, when Eric and Ernie were, for the first time in the Academy's history, the posthumous recipients of a lifetime achievement award and a place in BAFTA's Hall of Fame. That was quite a night. It wasn't just a case of Doreen Wise and my mother collecting the award – there followed a five-minute tribute to the work of Morecambe and Wise, through a montage of clips, and a standing ovation from a star-filled audience. Morecambe and Wise really were back!

I remember carrying the award back to the car afterwards and it weighed a ton. I kept getting sideways looks from people, and it was very easy to read in their eyes that they were thinking, 'Who the hell is he, and what did he do to get his hands on that?'

'Very little!' would have been my answer.

Later in the year, the whole family went up to Morecambe to watch the Queen unveiling a statue of EM in his home town. I arrived the previous evening with Tracey and the children, and checked into the hotel.

'Welcome to Morecambe, sir. Name, please?'

'Morecambe.'

'Sorry?'

'Morecambe. Gary Morecambe. Like the place.'

'Like here, you mean?'

'Yes.'

Eventually the receptionist wrote down my name, but whenever I have dealings with the town they always find it very hard to accept that I use the name. They understand that EM took it for his stage name, but that's as far as it goes.

Meeting us at the hotel were my mother, Gail and Steven. Gail's husband Jonathan and son Adam, from her first marriage, were there, too (Gail's daughter Amelia was 'down under' travelling). And there was Morecambe and Wise scriptwriter Eddie Braben, Frank Finlay, Sir Robin Day and many others. The hotel was right in the middle of the promenade, and the statue itself now stands directly in front of the very sands that EM had fished from as a child with his father. What a thought! 'One day, young lad, there's going to be a statue of you right here!'

The unveiling went by in a blur of excitement and pride. The morning started misty, but soon enough the sunshine broke through, crowds gathered, security tightened, and even the family had trouble getting close to the site of the ceremony prior to the arrival of the Queen and Prince Philip.

183

The ceremony was performed, and I think Her Majesty enjoyed the frivolity of it all, even if she did look a little bemused. 'Are you in the same line of work as your father?' she asked me. I should have said, 'Well, if I am, ma'am, I can't be much good, or you would have heard of me,' but I settled for 'No, ma'am, I'm a writer.' As the royal party departed, my son Henry started tap dancing, much to the amusement of the photographers. His picture monopolized the papers the next day. My youngest, Dereka, who was only four at the time, cried for most of the day, and had to be handed over to her godfather, Martin Sterling.

The statue is seven feet tall, cast in bronze by the very talented sculptor Graham Ibbeson. There are steps leading down from the figure to an area of ground where famous EM quotes have been engraved in stone, alongside a list of guest stars who appeared on *The Morecambe and Wise Show*. Before we left town we went to visit EM's former driver, Mike Fountain, and his wife Lesley, who lived in Morecambe. We sat in their front room drinking tea with EM's statue staring right back at us.

The following morning the whole Morecambe clan strolled down the promenade and bought fish and chips, which we ate near the shoreline. Sadie and George would have appreciated that simple touch.

In the years since the statue was erected people have said to me that Ernie should have been standing at EM's side. But the point was that the tribute wasn't about them as a double act – it was a tribute from Morecambe to its most famous son. Ernie didn't come from Morecambe, he came from Leeds, and he didn't adopt the name of his home town as his stage name. If there were a statue of the two of them, it should be outside BBC Television Centre in Wood Lane, where they made their greatest shows.

Funnily enough, I have come across statues of Eric and Ernie. Tracey and I took the children to Parnham House in Dorset, where we saw 15-foot fibreglass figures of Morecambe and Wise, with Eric slapping Ernie's cheeks as he did week in, week out on television. They were originally sculpted in the seventies as part of a tribute to British genius; they spent a short time in Regent's Park in London before being transferred to Sheffield, where they were defaced and generally abused. 'Typical of Sheffield,' EM joked at the time, which didn't go down too well with the inhabitants of the city.

After Sheffield all trace of the statues was lost until they turned up at Parnham House. When the owner sold up, he offered them to me for £25,000. If I'd had the money, I'd have bought them. Just recently a lady phoned and asked if I'd like to buy them for £5000 – she'd just found them standing up to their knees in mud in a farmer's field. Perhaps I'll own them one day.

Driving my son, Jack, home from a friend's house in Marlborough, I nearly swerved the car off the road when we stumbled across that very field. There stood Eric and Ernie in ironic grandeur dressed incongruously in dinner suit and black tie, with model Eric slapping model Ernie around the face. We pulled up and went to investigate. Apparently, the sculptor's daughter and her family live on the farm abutting the field. They have now acquired the statues and are contemplating what to do with them. To paraphrase EM, as their bases are filled with concrete I imagine the answer is 'not a lot'!

Even stranger was a discovery that Tracey made in a gift shop in Padstow, Cornwall: cruet sets of Eric and Ernie. I had to buy them. It would have been a quick process, but I noticed they'd spelt 'Morecambe' incorrectly; that sort of thing is a red rag to a bull. If you're going to merchandise someone's image – without permission, I might add – then at least spell the bloody name right. I didn't take the matter any further as I'm basically lazy. EM looks like the snooker player Dennis Taylor and Ernie looks like Edward Heath.

·

During those years of the Morecambe and Wise revival I was engaged in a number of different projects. Plans for the stage play kept rumbling along, but I had other projects too. I'd met Michael Sellers, the son of Peter Sellers, in 1996 and I knew that he'd written a book about his father, *PS I Love You*. Over a pint of cider in a pub in Hampstead, Michael shocked me by injecting himself at the table – with insulin, as he's diabetic. Shock over, we discussed a book on living with fame, which became *Hard Act to Follow*, an analysis of the effects on children of famous parents. I enjoyed working with Michael, because I was a big fan of Peter Sellers and I liked asking him questions about his father – it made such a change for me! It soon became clear that EM and Peter Sellers were very different people. Peter was unbelievably difficult, selfish, childish and unpredictable. I draw the line at using the word 'monster', because he didn't set out deliberately to hurt. The hurt was a by-product of all his other failings.

While we were working on the book Michael and I

discovered that, shortly before Peter's death, he and EM had talked about doing a book together. The idea was for Peter to take loads of photos of EM in various poses and guises, and then add funny captions. Eric and Ernie knew Peter quite well; they'd all done cameo parts in the 1970 movie *Simon, Simon*. In fact, the friendship went back even further than that, right back to the days when they were all treading the variety boards. When Peter's first marriage broke down, he shared his distraught state with my parents.

Peter Sellers was a great comic actor; he actually became the characters he portrayed. Mike showed me a picture of his father impersonating Adolf Hitler; the likeness is incredible, with a chilling deadness behind the eyes. EM was not like this. He was not an actor, for a start. And he always had the protection and support of a partner. Peter had an overwhelming, interfering mother. EM's life ran on safer, simpler rails. Mike said to me while we were working on the book, 'So, was your father virtually the same at home as he was on screen?' There was an element of surprise in his voice. 'Almost,' I said. I was faintly embarrassed by the recognition that EM was a comic icon without a trace of darkness in his personality.

•

Ernie Wise carried on working long after EM's death, but his career was, to all intents and purposes, over. He couldn't perform in another double act, although it was suggested that he could team up with Eric Sykes as another 'Eric and Ernie'. Nobody would have accepted that. Ernie realized that whatever he did after EM's death would have to be either very good or fairly low key, and he opted for the latter. He toured Australia with a one-man show that went down reasonably well, but soon he settled into the role of torchbearer for the double act. He did cruises, where he would recount memories of Morecambe and Wise: he'd talk about how they'd met, how they worked together, and he'd introduce screenings of their shows. He appeared on chat shows, he turned up to awards ceremonies, and he always got a great reception as the survivor of the nation's favourite double act. EM may have gone, but we still had Little Ern.

Ernie himself admitted, 'I feel a cold draught down one side where Eric used to be.' Without his partner he looked unprotected. His health deteriorated through the nineties, although he enjoyed life to the full. He died in March 1999. At his funeral in Maidenhead, Michael Grade's final words were: 'Thank you for all the laughter wot you gave us.' It was a simple, brilliant touch to sum up the joy that Morecambe and Wise brought into our lives.

•

Around this time I was invited down to Rose's Theatre in Tewkesbury – the very place where EM had collapsed and died – to attend a special screening of two Morecambe and Wise films, *The Intelligence Men* and *That Riviera Touch*. I arrived in the afternoon, so the local news teams could film me meandering melancholically across the stage. It was all rather contrived, but useful in diffusing the emotions I was going through, because I had to concentrate on their demands: 'Over here, Gary! Look this way, Gary! Walk slower, Gary! Look at the empty auditorium, Gary!' In a bizarre way I enjoyed it. Until that moment EM's death could have taken place in a different country – but here I was, just a two-and-a-half-hour car journey from home in the very place where he died. It was an undeniable fact and it had to be faced full on. I was also given a very exact description of the final moments, and I walked the final steps that my father had walked all those years earlier.

Later that evening I said a few words of welcome to the invited guests, one or two of whom had been in the audience that night in 1984. Then the theatre manager hung a picture of EM in a small conference suite named after him. The showing of the two films to a large and enthusiastic audience followed this, and in what seemed like no time at all I was back in my car heading south down the M5, my memories of my father's death redefined.

One footnote to this story: in the wake of poor returns the manager was asked to leave the theatre, and the Eric Morecambe picture – supplied by my mother – disappeared at the same moment.

chapter 16

In late summer 2001 the producer David Pugh rang me after seven years of silence to tell me that a play about Morecambe and Wise was ready to go. It was called *The Play What I Wrote*, it was written and performed by a double act called The Right Size – Sean Foley and Hamish McColl – and it was to be directed by Kenneth Branagh.

David had pulled off what Martin Sterling and I, and a long list of disgruntled or disappointed writers and directors, failed to do – he put together a play that serves as a tribute to Morecambe and Wise without directly impersonating them. I was amazed when he told me about it – and even more amazed when he asked me to become part of the team as the play's consultant. After years of frustration with the project, this was the perfect role for me; I was far too close to the subject to be involved in the writing, and I was a weary, creative blank after years of stop-go. The writers didn't need me; they had their own ideas, and they had a fair bit of new Eddie Braben material for good measure. My job was to see what was happening and to make suggestions, which would or wouldn't be taken on board. Martin Sterling had to move aside at this point; it was no longer the play we were working on. But we still work together, so there were no hard feelings.

I met the team for the first time in the rehearsal room, a church hall in Highbury, north London, and watched Kenneth Branagh putting them through their paces. Rehearsal stopped the moment I walked in; even David Pugh had only been allowed to see little bits of what they were preparing. We all went to the pub – Kenneth, his assistant director Michael, Sean, Hamish, David, Toby Jones – who played all the supporting roles – and me. Over beer and bacon sandwiches they filled me in on the play's progress – but not much. They were giving nothing away about the script; what went on in the rehearsal rooms was strictly behind closed doors. We talked in generalities, about what made Eric and Ernie tick, about EM's delivery: Kenneth pointed out that, like Robin Williams, Phil Silvers and Groucho Marx, EM had a sing-song voice, which could make the plainest lines seem very funny. Kenneth had clearly done his homework; he had a copy of *Behind the Sunshine* with him, which pleased me.

Hamish McColl, who loosely plays the Ernie character, told me that he had been dreading the moment of meeting me. He had expected me to be suspicious, questioning everything, interfering – but I'm none of those things. I have no point to prove or axe to grind. I enjoy representing the name of Eric Morecambe, but I'm not Eric Morecambe. God forbid that I should try to emulate, rather than just celebrate, my father.

The whole family loved the fact that someone of the calibre of Kenneth Branagh was directing a play about Morecambe and Wise: this was Henry V, Richard III, Ernest Shackleton, directing a play about 'a cheap music-hall act', as

EM would have put it. And his ambitions were big. 'I want this play not just to work,' he told me, 'but to be huge.' His wish would soon come true.

The previews began in Liverpool at the end of the summer. The first night was nerve-wracking because after months of careful planning we had no real idea of what the audience's reaction would be. It's a risky play; it's not directly about Morecambe and Wise, but about The Right Size, who slowly, magically, become Morecambe and Wise, without ever calling themselves anything but Sean and Hamish. The *coup de grâce* is the introduction of a guest star: in Liverpool, Michael Starkey took time out of *Brookside* to be the first hapless victim. The moment the guest star appears is sheer magic: the play suddenly takes flight, and this proved the key to its massive success. The guests changed with every few performances, and the reaction was very similar to the kind of joy that the real *Morecambe and Wise Show* used to give.

The previews were raw, lacking in some areas, over-cluttered in others. Some of the audience were in hysterics, others were totally bemused. One elderly man, clearly a big Morecambe and Wise fan, was purple with rage. 'This isn't Eric and Ernie! Where are they? We should demand our bloody money back!'

After the show we met up and discussed things. Ken was quick to point out that this was only a try-out, that there was still a lot of work to be done. When I got home the next day, I drew up six sides of paper with suggestions – including the key point, which was that you can't end a tribute to Morecambe and Wise without a rendition of their anthem, 'Bring Me Sunshine'. I assured Ken that it would take the roof off the place, and send the audience out with a smile on their face, humming the tune – and I was proved right. The song embodies everything that matters about Morecambe and Wise: sunshine, happiness, togetherness, innocence, making the world a happier place in which to live for 'each brand-new bright tomorrow'.

•

Three weeks later, we moved to Wyndham's Theatre on Charing Cross Road, slap bang in the West End of London. There were more previews, the script was sharper, and the performances took on greater depth. Toby, in particular, had been delving deeper into the role of Arthur Tolcher, the 'troubled' harmonica player from many a *Morecambe and Wise Show*. Ken, Sean and Hamish seemed very relaxed; David Pugh was restless, having difficulty keeping food down, and I felt a bit of a spare part, sending in last-minute thoughts, which were undoubtedly little more than a source of irritation as opening night loomed. Preview audiences were enthusiastic enough, particularly the younger ones. For the older ones, I sensed, there wasn't enough Eric and Ernie; some people wouldn't have been happy unless Eric and Ernie actually appeared in person.

Opening night at Wyndham's fell on 7 November 2001. My mother and our family, and Doreen Wise and hers, were all there, as were numerous famous faces including Ben Elton and Bruce Forsyth, whom I heard belly-laughing throughout the show. No one, particularly Ken, expected a standing ovation at the end. Hamish and Sean admitted that they'd reached a point in rehearsals where they just couldn't see it happening – but it did. There were endless rave reviews in the next day's papers. Bruce grabbed me on the way out and said, 'That was really fabulous. You must be so chuffed, Gary.'

We were euphoric, and utterly relieved. I walked away from that first night knowing that the image of Morecambe and Wise was not just intact, but enhanced. And at last I could walk away from that dreadful, nagging question: 'Will we ever get a Morecambe and Wise play up and running?'

From that opening night onwards the play pulled in big audiences and a host of famous names, from Steven Spielberg to the Sultan of Brunei, from Broadway producers to the Prince of Wales. And then there were the guest stars: Ralph Fiennes on the opening night, George Cole, Pierce Brosnan, Richard E. Grant, David Suchet, Roger Moore, Charles Dance, all of whom brought the house down. Dawn French was a particularly strong guest: she got a huge reaction when she stepped out on to the stage. She understood that it wasn't her job to be funny. 'In rehearsals,' she told me, 'I had this list of ideas that I showed to Ken. He looked at them, looked back at me and whispered, "No!" He was right of course – but there was a guillotine on stage, and I could have had such fun with that.'

Roger Moore gets the pat on the back for services given. He's guested over forty times. When I met him after one of his earlier appearances he made it very clear what his motivation is. 'You see, Gary, I always wanted to be a guest star on *The Morecambe and Wise Show*, but we were usually shooting the Bond movies around the same time and could never get it together.' So Roger's living that moment by proxy and loving every moment despite a dip in his health when he collapsed on stage during a Broadway performance.

The Play What I Wrote ran at the Wyndham's until May 2002 and won an Olivier Award for Best New Play. Toby Jones won Best Supporting Actor. I saw the awards on TV, and was very moved when Hamish, accepting his award, said, 'I dedicate this to Eric and Ernie.' It was revived at Wyndham's in November 2002, with Roger Moore as the guest star, and an audience that included David Suchet, Eric Idle, Twiggy, Eddie Izzard and Angela Rippon. There was one big change: Sean and Hamish now had a shower in their dressing room, courtesy of Madonna – who had just been performing at the Wyndham's.

I must mention the man who choreographed the play. Irving Davies first met Morecambe and Wise in 1943, when they were appearing in *Strike a New Note*; at the time of the opening he was their oldest living associate. Nobody went back that far, not even my mother! On the opening night of the revival I was hunting around the foyer for Irving and asked Sean where he was.

'Haven't you heard?'

'What?'

'Irving collapsed and died while we were previewing in Newcastle a few weeks back. He was absolutely fine, then he had a massive heart attack and was dead before he hit the floor.'

Irving was a sensitive man who had a real affinity with Morecambe and Wise. He once told me as we stood at the back of the Wyndham's Theatre, 'I can feel Eric and Ernie's presence in this auditorium. It's as if they're here.'

At the time of writing *The Play What I Wrote* continues from strength to strength. It's up for a Tony award for the Broadway production, and this autumn will return to the UK, probably as a touring production.

•

So where does all this leave me – the son of a famous father whose working life is still dominated by that relationship? My role now is as a sounding board for anything concerning Morecambe and Wise, and with the continuing growth of interest in the subject I'm more in demand than ever. Fortunately for me, it's a role I can switch on and off. EM could never switch off the role of Eric Morecambe; he and his family had to live with that all the time, which could be extremely burdensome. The fact that I don't is a great release – and it's made me understand, more than I ever did during EM's lifetime, how tiring it must have been to be Eric Morecambe.

Writing this book has been a cathartic venture for me. I've talked about doing it for years, and I've avoided doing it for years. I've written about Morecambe and Wise several times, but I've never fully studied my relationship with my father until now. This time, as the American films say, it's personal. Perhaps it's a kind of therapy. The word therapy always made me shudder, but now I can see it as part of a wider process of coming to terms with what the world throws at you. While I was writing this book, my marriage ended: Tracey and I have gone our separate ways after twenty-two years. After complaining for so long that my father was absent for large parts of my childhood, I'm now going to be absent from my own children's lives; I can't be there for them as often as they would like. I'm in therapy as a way of dealing with that, and to my surprise I like it. It's therapeutic, believe it or not.

It's nearly twenty years since EM died, and I've had a lot of time in which to grow up and get things into perspective. I'm no longer a lonely twenty-five-year-old sitting at home with some axe to grind. I know that's how the media like to portray the children of famous people, but there's more to us than that. I've had a chance to distance myself from EM, and to realize that there are many different aspects to my character – being the son of Eric Morecambe is only one of them.

I don't use the Morecambe name all the time; in my private life, I'm often plain old Gary Bartholomew. Mind you, anonymity doesn't always pay. I was on holiday in Cornwall once with my mother and friends, and I'd booked a table at Rick Stein's restaurant in Padstow. He's a Morecambe and Wise fan – he opened one of his TV shows on Morecambe Bay, in front of EM's statue – and my mother is a fan of his. The idea of a bit of mutual admiration seemed rather attractive. We were all enjoying our meal, and Rick was floating in and out of the restaurant, not saying a word to us. When we got home, there was a message on the answering machine from Rick, hugely apologetic.

'I looked through the reservations, but I couldn't see any party booked in the name of Morecambe, so I presumed you weren't there.'

Never mind, Rick. We'll be back.

afterword

The hotel is unknown to me, yet somehow familiar. It is large and perched on a cliff top overlooking a beach, where the weather is good and people sunbathe and play at the water's edge. All indications are this isn't England. It is a hotel one can easily lose oneself in, and I do – frequently.

EM is trying to be his old self. I am background material, fully conscious that the 'old self' he portrays is from a distant, happier past. And yet he is struggling to entertain the people who are trying to talk with him and who are enjoying being in his company. I know this to be so because that is how it always was with him, but I sense that it is no longer so easy. Nevertheless, I also know that he is dead. No one else knows that he is dead, and as the dream progresses, I'm uncertain whether EM realizes it himself. When we separate ourselves from the crowds and head for the restaurant, many stairways and lift rides away, no mention of life or death, past or present, is made. It strikes me that I know I'm dreaming, and this dream is designed to deal with conversations that the suddenness of EM's death denied me: but I ignore this explanation, preferring to believe that it is real and it is now.

'Be careful,' I warn him. 'Don't walk so quickly. You must take care of yourself.'

He nods, but now I'm fairly sure he doesn't know he's dead, because he's walking quickly and smoking a cigarette. He wouldn't be able to do the latter if he were dead, and the former is somehow incongruous with a visiting spirit.

The restaurant is large and plush. We settle down to eat together, and I begin to see where the dream is taking me. 'You'll be fine in the show tonight,' he remarks, as if referring to a previous conversation.

'Yes, I suppose so,' I answer.

Then we leave the restaurant, the food untouched, and we are side-stage of a theatre. EM is using the peephole to check on the audience – which is how it was in real life – and the auditorium is steadily filling. I feel my heartbeat increase as I realize what's about to take place. I find a dressing-room and start glancing at piles of scripts that all have the name of Ernie Wise upon them, for that is my purpose – I am to be my father's straight man.

Then the stage manager summons us. I'm thinking that EM shouldn't be doing this stuff as it's killed him once already, but he turns to me unfazed. He seems to feel that I can cope with Ernie's role, but I know that he doesn't know that I haven't even seen a script, let alone learned one.

But it's too late, and the audience applaud, and I feel a push between my shoulder blades. As I stumble onto the stage I feel a wave of relief wash over me as I awake from my recurring dream.

chronology
The Morecambe and Wise Show

The Morecambe and Wise Show (ATV)

Series 1

12 October 1961	Jack Parnell and His Orchestra
19 October 1961	The Confederates
26 October 1961	Acker Bilk
2 November 1961	The McGuire Sisters
9 November 1961	The Peters Sisters
16 November 1961	Cleo Laine
23 November 1961	Gary Miller
30 November 1961	Mickie Ashmon's Ragtime Jazz Band, Valerie Masters
7 December 1961	The Kaye Sisters

Series 2

30 June 1962	Terry Lightfoot's Jazzmen, The Kaye Sisters
7 July 1962	Kenny Ball's Jazzmen, The Beverley Sisters
14 July 1962	Alex Welsh and His Band, The Beverley Sisters
21 July 1962	Acker Bilk, The Beverley Sisters

28 July 1962	The Mike Cotton Jazzmen, Susan Maughan
4 August 1962	Chris Barber's Jazzband, Ottilie Patterson, The Beverley Sisters
11 August 1962	The Clyde Valley Stompers, The Beverley Sisters
18 August 1962	Eric Delaney and His Band, Teddy Johnson and Pearl Carr
25 August 1962	George Chisholm's Jazz Gang, Teddy Johnson and Pearl Carr
1 September 1962	Humphrey Lyttelton and His Band, Lita Roza
8 September 1962	Alex Welsh and His Band, Janice Marden
15 September 1962	The Mike Cotton Jazzmen, Teddy Johnson and Pearl Carr
22 September 1962	Jack Parnell and His Debonaires, Teddy Johnson and Pearl Carr

Series 3

15 June 1963	Joe Brown and His Bruvvers, The Michael Sammes Singers
22 June 1963	Acker Bilk, The Michael Sammes Singers
29 June 1963	The King Brothers, Barbara Law, Murray Kash
6 July 1963	Sheila Buxton, The Michael Sammes Singers
13 July 1963	The King Brothers, Janice Marden
20 July 1963	The King Brothers, Susan Maughan

27 July 1963	The King Brothers, Sheila Southern
3 August 1963	Roy Castle
10 August 1963	Shani Wallis, The Michael Sammes Singers
17 August 1963	The King Brothers, Maureen Evans
24 August 1963	The King Brothers, Kathy Kirby
31 August 1963	Eric Delaney's Band, Lucille Gaye
7 September 1963	The King Brothers, Rosemary Squires

Series 4

4 April 1964	Eddie Calvert and the 'C' Men, The Raindrops
11 April 1964	Janice Marden, Yvonne Antrobus, Kenny Ball
18 April 1964	The Beatles
25 April 1964	Chris Rayburn, The Viscounts, Pearl Lane, Janet Webb
2 May 1964	Jackie Trent, Penny Morrell, Yvonne Antrobus, Freddie Powell, Acker Bilk
9 May 1964	Patsy Ann Noble, The Fraser Hayes Four, Sally Williams, Janet Webb
16 May 1964	Sheila Buxton, Alan Curtis, Yvonne Antrobus, Edmund Hockridge
23 May 1964	The King Brothers, Freddie Powell, Kathy Kirby, Marilyn Gothard, Janet Webb
30 May 1964	Joe Brown and the Bruvvers, Joy Marshall, Pearl Lane, Jeannette Bradbury

6 June 1964	Four Macs, Jo Williamson, Dickie Valentine
13 June 1964	Valerie Masters, Gladys Whitehead, Alan Curtis, Jo Williamson, The Bachelors
20 June 1964	Ray Ellington, Barbara Law, Penny Morrell
27 June 1964	The Migil 5, Sandra Boize, Jo Williamson, Sally Douglas, Thelma Taylor, Valerie Van Ost, Christina Wass, Julie Devonshire, Susan Maughan

Series 5

22 January 1966	Lulu, Paul and Barry Ryan
29 January 1966	Morgan James Duo
5 February 1966	Jackie Trent, The New Faces
12 February 1966	Millicent Martin
19 February 1966	Georgie Fame and the Blue Flames, Julie Rogers
26 February 1966	The Settlers, Barbara Law
5 March 1966	The King Brothers
12 March 1966	The Shadows, Janice Marden
19 March 1966	Herman's Hermits, Teddy Johnson and Pearl Carr

Series 6

1 October 1967	Millicent Martin, Freddie & the Dreamers
22 October 1967	Millicent Martin, The Small Faces, Bobby Rydell
12 November 1967	Millicent Martin, The Hollies, Tom Jones

10 December 1967	Millicent Martin, Manfred Mann, George Maharis
4 February 1968	Millicent Martin, The Tremeloes, Peter Nero
25 February 1968	Millicent Martin, Eric Burdon and the Animals, Gene Pitney
17 March 1968	Millicent Martin, Georgie Fame, Bobby Vinton
31 March 1968	Millicent Martin, The Dave Clark Five, Cliff Richard

The Morecambe & Wise Show (BBC)

Series 1 (BBC2)

2 September 1968	Georgia Brown, Los Zafiros, Jenny Lee-Wright, Bettine Le Beau, Kenny Ball and His Jazzmen
9 September 1968	Acker Bilk, Jenny Lee-Wright, Sheila Bernette, Caron Gardner, Bettine Le Beau, Judy Robinson, Tina Martin, Jenny Russell
16 September 1968	Trio Athenee, The Paper Dolls, Jenny Lee-Wright, Jimmy Lee, Kenny Ball, Ann Hamilton
23 September 1968	Bruce Forsyth, Kenny Ball, Jenny Lee-Wright, Ann Hamilton
30 September 1968	Ronnie Carroll, Kenny Ball, Jenny Lee-Wright, Michele Barrie, Jane Bartlett, Wendy Hillhouse, Bebe Robson

7 October 1968	Edmund Hockridge, Kenny Ball, Ann Hamilton
14 October 1968	Michael Aspel, Chris Langford, Kenny Ball, Jimmy Berryman, Lesley Roach, Ann Hamilton, Jenny Lee-Wright
21 October 1968	Matt Monro, Kenny Ball, Ann Hamilton

Series 2 (BBC2)

27 July 1969	Peter Cushing, Bobbie Gentry, Vince Hill, Kenny Ball, Ann Hamilton, Janet Webb, Constance Carling, Diana Powell
10 August 1969	Trio Athenee, Malcolm Roberts, Ann Hamilton, Janet Webb
24 August 1969	Juliet Mills, Moira Anderson, Ann Hamilton, The Pattersons, Kenny Ball, Janet Webb, Lynda Thomas
7 September 1969	Edward Woodward, Kenneth McKellar, Ann Hamilton, The Pattersons, Kenny Ball, Rex Rashley, Karen Birch, Richard Scott, Janet Webb
25 December 1969	Susan Hampshire, Frankie Vaughan, Nina, Ann Hamilton, Janet Webb

Series 3 (BBC2)

14 January 1970	Herman's Hermits, Ann Hamilton, Janet Webb
28 January 1970	Ian Carmichael, Nina, Ann Hamilton, Janet Webb
11 February 1970	Fenella Fielding, Sacha Distel, Ann Hamilton, Janet Webb

11 March 1970	Diane Cilento, Vince Hill, Deryck Guyler, Ann Hamilton, Janet Webb
25 March 1970	Edward Chapman, Clodagh Rogers, Nanette, Ann Hamilton, Janet Webb
8 April 1970	Nina Golden, Ann Hamilton, Janet Webb
22 April 1970	Richard Greene, Nana Mouskouri, Ann Hamilton, Janet Webb

Series 4 (BBC2)

1 July 1970	Eric Porter, Jan Daley, Trio Athenee, Ann Hamilton, Janet Webb
15 July 1970	Kenneth McKellar, George A. Cooper, Margery Mason, Samantha Jones, Ann Hamilton, Janet Webb
29 July 1970	Nina, Craig Douglas, Ann Hamilton, Jenny Lee-Wright, Janet Webb
12 August 1970	Fenella Fielding, Ray Stevens, Sylvia McNeil, Ann Hamilton, Janet Webb
26 August 1970	Barbara Murray, Dusty Springfield, Michael Redgrave, Robin Day, Ann Hamilton, Janet Webb
25 December 1970	Peter Cushing, William Franklyn, Nina, Eric Porter, Edward Woodward, Ann Hamilton, Alan Curtis, Rex Rashley, Janet Webb

Series 5 (BBC1)

8 April 1971	Flora Robson, Esther Ofarim, Peter & Alex, Kenny Ball, Ann Hamilton, Alan Curtis, David March, Janet Webb
22 April 1971	Robert Young, Susan Maughan, the entire *Dad's Army* cast, Ann Hamilton, Janet Webb
6 May 1971	Frank Ifield, The Settlers, Ann Hamilton, Kenny Ball, Richard Caldicot, Michael Ward, Gordon Clyde, Grazina Frame, Brychan Powell, Janet Webb
20 May 1971	Jack Jones, Sheila Southern, Ann Hamilton, Kenny Ball, Gordon Clyde, Grazina Frame, Frank Tregear, Arthur Tolcher, Lillian Padmore, Michael Mulcaster, Stanley Mason, Janet Webb
3 June 1971	Glenda Jackson, Mary Hopkin, Ronnie Hilton, Ann Hamilton, Janet Webb
17 June 1971	Ian Carmichael, Matt Monro, Kiki Dee, Peter & Alex, Ann Hamilton, Janet Webb
15 July 1971	Trio Athenee, Kenny Ball, Ann Hamilton, Design, Rex Rashley, Gerald Case, Janet Webb

Series 6 (BBC1)

19 September 1971	Francis Matthews, Anita Harris, Robert Young, Ann Hamilton, Janet Webb

26 September 1971	Keith Michell, Design, Ann Hamilton, Janet Webb
3 October 1971	Cilla Black, Connie Carroll, Percy Thrower, Ann Hamilton, Janet Webb
10 October 1971	John Mills, Mrs Mills, Trio Athenee, Ann Hamilton, Kenny Ball, Arnold Diamond, Tony Melody, Janet Webb
17 October 1971	Nina, The Pattersons, Kenny Ball, Ann Hamilton, Christine Shaw, Frank Tregear, Janet Webb
31 October 1971	Tom Jones, Design, Ann Hamilton, Kenny Ball, Gordon Clyde, Rex Rashley, Janet Webb
25 December 1971	Shirley Bassey, Glenda Jackson, Francis Matthews, André Previn, Ann Hamilton, Los Zafiros, Kenneth Hendel, Rex Rashley, Arthur Tolcher, Ken Alexis, Dick Emery, Frank Bough, Robert Dougall, Cliff Michelmore, Patrick Moore, Michael Parkinson, Eddie Waring, Janet Webb
25 December 1972	Glenda Jackson, Jack Jones, Vera Lynn, Pete Murray, Shirley Bassey, André Previn, Ann Hamilton, Kenny Ball, Ian Carmichael, Fenella Fielding, Eric Porter, Flora Robson, Janet Webb

Series 7 (BBC1)

5 January 1973	Cliff Richard, Vikki Carr, Ann Hamilton
12 January 1973	Robert Morley, Vicky Leandros, Ann Hamilton, New World
19 January 1973	Lulu, Rostal Schaefer, Henry Cooper, Ann Hamilton
26 January 1973	Susan Hampshire, Georgie Fame, Alan Price, Ann Hamilton, The Settlers
2 February 1973	Frank Finlay, Wilma Reading, Ann Hamilton, Design
9 February 1973	Helen Reddy, Alex Welsh and His Band
16 February 1973	Anita Harris, Reg Lye, Anthony Sharp, Ann Hamilton
23 February 1973	Wilma Reading, Ann Hamilton, Springfield Revival
2 March 1973	Hannah Gordon, Mary Travers, Christopher Neil, Ann Hamilton, Raymond Mason, Hatti Riemer, Anthony Sharp, Christine Shaw
9 March 1973	Roy Castle, Pete Murray, Anna Murphy, Ann Hamilton, The Pattersons
16 March 1973	Nana Mouskouri, The Black and White Minstrels, Harry Corbett and Sooty, George Hamilton IV, Ann Hamilton
23 March 1973	Peter Cushing, Wilma Reading, Alan Price, Ann Hamilton
25 December 1973	Vanessa Redgrave, Hannah Gordon, John Hanson, The New Seekers, Yehudi Menuhin, Rudolf Nureyev, Laurence Olivier, André Previn, Ann Hamilton

Series 8 (BBC1)

27 September 1974	André Previn, Magnus Magnusson, Mrs Mills, Ann Hamilton, Wilma Reading, Arthur Tolcher
4 October 1974	Ludovic Kennedy, Wilma Reading, Ann Hamilton
11 October 1974	The Syd Lawrence Orchestra, Wilma Reading, Ann Hamilton
18 October 1974	Richard Baker, Wilma Reading, Ann Hamilton
25 October 1974	Hughie Green, David Dimbleby, Wilma Reading, Ann Hamilton
1 November 1974	June Whitfield, Wilma Reading, Ann Hamilton
25 December 1975	Diana Rigg, Des O'Connor, Gordon Jackson, Robin Day, Ann Hamilton

Series 9 (BBC1)

7 January 1976	Peter O'Sullivan, Gilbert O'Sullivan, Dilys Watling, The Vernons, Arthur Tolcher
14 January 1976	Michele Dotrice, Frankie Vaughan, Patrick Moore
11 February 1976	Lena Zavaroni, The Spinners, Allan Cuthbertson, Ann Hamilton
10 March 1976	Jackie Damell, Allan Cuthbertson, Anthony Sharp, Ann Hamilton
24 March 1976	The Karlins, Vincent Zarra, Ann Hamilton

19 April 1976	Diane Solomon, Champagne, Maggie Fitzgibbon, Ann Hamilton
25 December 1976	Elton John, Angela Rippon, John Thaw, Dennis Waterman, Kate O'Mara, Marion Montgomery, The Nolans
25 December 1977	Penelope Keith, Elton John, Francis Matthews, Arthur Lowe, John Le Mesurier, John Laurie, Richard Briers, Paul Eddington, Angharad Rees, Stella Starr, Angela Rippon, Michael Aspel, Richard Baker, Frank Bough, Philip Jenkinson, Kenneth Kendall, Barry Norman, Eddie Waring, Richard Whitmore, Peter Woods, Sandra Dainty, Jenny Lee-Wright, Valerie Leon

The Morecambe and Wise Show (THAMES)

Specials

18 October 1978	Donald Sinden, Judi Dench, Leonard Sachs, Peter Cushing, Derek Griffiths, Ann Hamilton, Kenneth Watson, The Syd Lawrence Orchestra
25 December 1978	Leonard Rossiter, Frank Finlay, Harold Wilson, Jenny Hanley, Anna Dawson, Frank Coda, Jan Hunt, Jilliane Foot
25 December 1979	David Frost, Glenda Jackson, Des O'Connor

Series 1

3 September 1980	Terry Wogan, Ann Hamilton
10 September 1980	Hannah Gordon, Hugh Paddick, Frank Coda
17 September 1980	Dave Prowse, Anthony Chinn, Raymond Mason, Fiesta Mei Ling
24 September 1980	Deryck Guyler, Gerald Case
1 October 1980	Suzanne Danielle, Valerie Minifie
8 October 1980	Gemma Craven
25 December 1980	Peter Barkworth, Peter Cushing, Jill Gascoigne, Alec Guinness, Peter Vaughan, Gemma Craven

Series 2

1 September 1981	Gemma Craven, Kate Lock, Kay Korda
8 September 1981	Richard Vernon
15 September 1981	Diane Keen
22 September 1981	George Chisholm
29 September 1981	Peter Bowles, Suzanne Danielle, Faith Brown, April Walker
6 October 1981	Robert Hardy, Ian Ogilvy, Kay Korda
13 October 1981	Joanna Lumley, Richard Vernon
23 December 1981	Ralph Richardson, Robert Hardy, Suzannah York

Series 3

27 October 1982	Richard Briers, Diana Dors, Bonnie Langford, Peter Salmon
3 November 1982	Trevor Eve, Wayne Sleep, Jimmy Young, Penny Meredith

10 November 1982   Roy Castle, Peter Salmon
17 November 1982   Colin Welland, Isla St Clair
24 November 1982   Patricia Brake, Royce Mills
1 December 1982   Alan Dobie, Marian Montgomery, Kay Korda
8 December 1982   Nigel Hawthorne, Patricia Brake
27 December 1982   Robert Hardy, Rula Lenska, Richard Vernon, Wall Street Crash, Diana Dors, Denis Healey, Glenda Jackson, André Previn, Jimmy Young

Series 4
7 September 1983   Margaret Courtenay, Anna Dawson, Maggie Moone
14 September 1983   David Keman, Jenny Lee-Wright
21 September 1983   Cherry Gillespie, Anita Graham, Penny Meredith
28 September 1983   Stutz Bear Cats, Denise Kelly
5 October 1983   Cherry Gillespie, Anita Graham, Penny Meredith
12 October 1983   Margaret Courtenay, Stutz Bear Cats, Peter & Jackie Fimani
19 October 1983   Harry Fowler, Peter Finn, Valerie Minifie
26 December 1983   Gemma Craven, Nigel Hawthorne, Derek Jacobi, Felicity Kendal, Burt Kwouk, Tony Monopoly, Fulton Mackay, Jennie Linden, Patrick Mower, Nanette Newman, Peter Skellern

Movies

The Intelligence Men (US: Spylarks), Rank, 1965

Director	Robert Asher
Screenplay	Sid Green and Dick Hills, based on a story by Peter Blackmore
Cinematography	Jack Asher
Editor	Gerry Hambling
Cast	Eric Morecambe, Ernie Wise, William Franklyn, Terence Alexander, Francis Matthews, April Olrich, Gloria Paul, Richard Vernon, David Lodge, Jacqueline Jones, Warren Mitchell, Brian Oulton, Michael Peake, Peter Bull, Tutte Lemkow, Rene Sartoris, Graham Smith, Dilys Rosser, Johnny Briggs, Elizabeth Counsell, Gerard Hely, Joe Melia, George Roderick
Running Time	104 minutes.

That Riviera Touch, Rank, 1966

Director	Cliff Owen
Screenplay	Sid Green, Dick Hills and Peter Blackmore, based on a story by Peter Blackmore
Cinematography	Otto Heller
Editor	Gerry Hambling
Cast	Eric Morecambe, Ernie Wise, Suzanne Lloyd, Paul Stassino, Armand Mestral, George Eugeniou, George Pastell,

215

Peter Jeffrey, Gerald Lawson, Michael
Forrest, Clive Cazes, Steven Scott, Paul
Danquah, Francis Matthews, Alexandra
Bastedo, Nicole Shelby

Running Time   98 minutes.

The Magnificent Two (US: What Happened at Campo Grande), Rank, 1967

Director   Cliff Owen
Screenplay   Sid Green, Dick Hills, Michael Pertwee
                  and Peter Blackmore, based on a story
                  by Michael Pertwee
Cinematography Ernest Steward
Editor   Gerry Hambling
Cast   Eric Morecambe, Ernie Wise, Margit
                  Saad, Virgilio Teixeira, Cecil Parker,
                  Isobel Black, Martin Benson, Michael
                  Godfrey, Sue Sylvaine, Henry Beltran,
                  Tyler Butterworth, Sandor Eles, Andreas
                  Malandrinos, Victor Maddern, Michael
                  Gover, Charles Laurence, Larry Taylor,
                  David Charlesworth, Hugo De Vernier,
                  Sara Luzita, Bettine Le Beau, Aubrey
                  Morris, Carlos Douglas, Anna Gilchrist,
                  Catherine Griller
Running Time   100 minutes.

216

Simon, Simon, Denouement Films/Shillingford Associates, 1970

Director	Graham Stark
Screenplay	Graham Stark
Cinematographers	Derek Vanlint, Harvey Harrison
Editor	Bunny Warren
Cast	Graham Stark, John Junkin, Julia Foster, Norman Rossington, Kenneth Earl, David Hemmings, Paul Whitsun-Jones, Peter Sellers, Michael Caine, Eric Morecambe, Ernie Wise, Bernie Winters, Bob Monkhouse, Pete Murray, Tony Blackburn, Tommy Godfrey
Running Time	30 minutes

Night Train to Murder, Euston Films, 1985

Director	Joe McGrath
Screenplay	Morecambe and Wise and Joe McGrath, based on an idea by Morecambe and Wise
Cinematography	Adrian Fearnley
Editor	Dave Lewington
Cast	Eric Morecambe, Ernie Wise, Lysette Anthony, Fulton Mackay, Roger Brierly, Pamela Salem, Kenneth Haigh, Richard Vernon, Edward Judd, Ben Aris, Tony Boncza, Frank Coda, Robert Longden, Penny Meredith, Tim Stern, Zoe Nicholas, Michelle Tascher
Running Time	79 minutes.

index